**The Keeper of the Laugh**
Danny Fromchenko

Producer & International Distributor
eBookPro Publishing
www.ebook-pro.com

**The Keeper of the Laugh**
**Danny Fromchenko**

Translation: Lisa Namdar Kaufman

Contact: danny@auto.co.il
ISBN : 9798365860735

# THE KEEPER
# OF THE LAUGH

DANNY FROMCHENKO

# Prologue

Max sat looking in the mirror, just as he had thousands of times over the previous years, seeing-not-seeing the eyes that stared back at him. The cheers of the merry audience, the thunder of the drums, the blare of the trumpets, and the low oompah of the tubas - none of it penetrated the wall insulating his senses.

At that moment, his entire world was focused on the one repetitive action he executed once, sometimes twice a day, day after day, week after week, year after year. Using a tiny key, he wound the spring in the back of the tin clown in front of him. When he finished, he put the clown down on the table and it began to beat a tin drum slung from its belt.

Max pulled a bald wig encircled with a snarl of pink cotton over his head. He carefully spread a thick layer of white paint on his face. With a thin brush, he painted two high semi-circles, black as coal, for eyebrows, added black liner around his eyes, a large mouth, wide and smiling, and a big beauty mark on his right cheek.

He put down the brush and looked in the mirror. Staring-not-staring at him was a white figure with a smile of surprise or wonder. It was impossible to know whether Max and the character he faced were pleased or displeased with the sight before them.

Exactly like the wind-up clown, beating his little tin drum with his right hand and then his left, Max continued his work automatically. Without glancing at the tin clown, who at that moment had exhausted his energy, Max began to paint his eyelids a glittering blue. Finally, it was time for the red, a color a clown clearly cannot do without. He painted wide, red lines around his lips, drawing them far from the edges of his mouth.

In precise concert with the moment he put down the red brush, the excited call of the ring master could be heard in the background, "Please welcome the funniest clown in the world, the man who has made more children laugh than anyone else in history. No one knows from where he came or to where he is going... H e r e' s... A n o n y m o u s!"

Max thrust his hand out at the tin clown and knocked him onto his face, covered his own nose with a red rubber ball, stood up, and strode towards the circus ring. The roar of the crowd, the cheers of the children, and the sounds of the noisy circus orchestra reached his ears. But through it all, in the background, from some undefined direction, he also heard the sound that accompanied him day and night, through wakefulness and dreams, the sound that never let up: pealing wails of crazy laughter like only a hyena in heat could make - deep in her throat, in the dark of night.

With every step that brought him closer to the ring, Max grew lighter, more flexible. He moved like a dancer, or more like a shark, in perpetual, effortless motion, while his cold, dead eyes focused on his prey.

From the moment Anonymous burst into the rollicking circus ring – nothing was left of Max – even the crazy laugh was nearly silenced. Except for the dead eyes that ceaselessly scanned the crowd as if searching for something lost, there was barely anything that connected Max to Anonymous the Clown, who elicited howls of laughter and tears of joy with the skill of an artist.

And that is exactly what made Anonymous the very best of clowns. He knew how to listen to the crowd while moving, to feel what would awaken something in them and open them to laughing out loud – and what would shut them down and lead to cynical chuckles. And, therefore, Anonymous was unlike any other clown falling face-down in the circus tent.

But why should this come as a surprise to any of you, dear readers? No other clown, before or after, knew with such complete certainty that life and death were dependent on his ability to make someone laugh.

# July 1945, Munich

About a month after the Germans surrendered to American armed forces, a black Mercedes came to a stop next to the entrance of the American command in Munich. A tall, light-haired woman emerged from the passenger side door. She wore a light grey button-down linen shirt that emphasized her shoulders, a knee-length skirt, and a string of large pearls around her neck. Her long legs and black pumps both added to her look and to the authority she radiated.

Despite her height, she was dwarfed by the man who got out of the driver's side door. He wore a beige perfectly tailored suit and a red tie and towered over her by more than a head. When he stood beside her, his broad back and shoulders looked like a frame wrapped around her thin body. He presented an invitation and his ID to the guard at the gate, where the woman was also required to identify herself.

The guard opened the gate and directed them where to go in carefully enunciated and absurdly slow English. Alexandra and Iron were used to Americans speaking that way to everyone who wasn't American, even when they were addressed in English.

Their destination was the "Department for Locating Family Members from Concentration Camps in Areas Under American Control." A polite, young officer sat behind a desk and, without any extraneous preamble said, "I understand, Mrs. Brecholdt that you're looking for the Jewish theater actor who was held at Camp A32, as we refer to it, in Kaufering, Bavaria, from an unknown date until liberation."

"I don't know if he's still alive, but I do know that about two months ago he was alive and well."

"Do you have evidence of that?"

"Yes, we were there and we saw him, my partner, Mr. Iron Mensch and I." Alexandra pointed towards the giant man who nodded lightly.

"And what is your relation to Mr. Fischer? Apparently, he is a Jew and in your German identification card, it says..."

"I know what it says in my German identification card," Alexandra snapped disdainfully. "He was my colleague and mentor at the Shakespearean Theater in Berlin."

"I'm sorry, ma'am, I'm not sure I can help you. We're the Department for Locating Family Members, family only."

"Is he alive? Is he well? Do you know where he is?" Alexandra couldn't hide the panic and desperation that crept into her voice.

"Sorry," said the young man, the tone of his voice betraying that the subject was as close to his heart as his hometown of Montgomery, Alabama was to where he sat. "I have to check if the matter is under my authority."

A knock on the door interrupted their conversation. A young female soldier entered the room and, without a word, handed the officer a note. He glanced at it, pressed a button installed on his desk, and turned to Iron.

"Are you Iron Mensch?"

Iron was surprised by the change of subject and looked into the officer's eyes. What he saw was a hunter locking onto his prey, and realized that he, himself, was that prey.

"Yes," he answered calmly.

The door opened and two uniformed soldiers entered with their guns drawn.

"You're wanted for questioning in connection with your service in the Gestapo," the officer said. And before Alexandra had a chance to respond, Iron stood up. The soldiers, threatened by his size, rushed to point their weapons at him.

"Relax, I'll come with you for questioning, I have nothing to hide."

"He was only a driver!" Alexandra yelled.

"It says here that he murdered two people!" The officer waved the note in his hand.

Alexandra looked at Iron in shock. "He has the softest heart of anyone I've ever known, what are you talking about?"

Iron smiled at her. "Don't worry. Everything will be cleared up quickly. Just convince the officer to arrange a meeting for you with Max, and I'll be back here before you know it." Although he sounded confident, Iron had no idea what he might be facing. The three exited the room without another word.

"I'm sorry," said the officer. "We must investigate whatever information we have about SS members. As for Fischer, I'll check if I have the authority to grant you permission to see him."

Alexandra was silent a moment. "And if I tell you that I'm the mother of his child?" she asked. The officer flipped quickly through the papers before him. He looked perturbed. "You said you're the mother of his child, ma'am?" He picked up the receiver of the telephone on his desk and asked the operator to have Dr. David Greenberg come to his office immediately.

Silence reigned. After a few moments, the phone rang. The officer listened, then turned to Alexandra and asked if she could come back the next day, it was important that Dr. Greenberg meet her.

Alexandra nodded and asked how she could see Iron.

"He was taken for questioning, which usually ends within the day and without arrest. If you have a telephone at home, I promise to update you personally about his situation.

"I can't go home without my driver," she said.

The officer answered that he was unable to help her and asked her to wait outside his office.

With no other option, Alexandra waited outside the room and read through a colorful issue of LIFE magazine with amazement. She was sure Iron would return. And indeed, several hours later, he did so in a good mood.

"Good people, these Americans," he said cheerfully. "Their behavior is so different from the Germans, and still the animals within them are so similar."

"Did you murder two people, Iron?! You?!"

"I didn't exactly murder them, Alexandra. They were SS men who deserved to die. I explained it to the Americans, and I'll explain it all to you, too, at home. But more importantly, what did I miss here?"

"We're coming back tomorrow. I'm supposed to meet a doctor named Greenberg."

"Good news, no?"

"Let's hope so," said Alexandra and stood up.

"Did you give Franz's envelope to the American?" asked Iron.

"No, I saved it as a bargaining chip in case they didn't give you back to me. Now, I'll give it to him."

She knocked on the officer's door and entered the room quickly. Before he was able to open his mouth, she took the sealed envelope from her bag and placed it on his desk. "I have a gift for you. The personal diary of Franz Schmidt, the Gestapo commander in Bavaria. I won't tell you how it came into my possession. I assume it will help you catch fatter fish than a little minnow like Iron Mensch."

The officer took the diary and looked at it. "It's in German."

"If you didn't know, the Gestapo wrote in German," spit Alexandra.

"Can you translate something from it for me, please?"

"No. I don't want to see a single word of what's written there. It's explosive material. You ought to get it to your commanders, they'll know what to do with it."

# 1936, Berlin

Franz Schmidt, the Gestapo commander in the central district of Berlin, leaned back in his chair and sighed with satisfaction. He loved solving mysteries and arresting criminals. It was in his blood. He was talented, cultured, and a supporter of the arts. He was not cruel and didn't even hate Jews. Despite being under the command of the SS, he hated the low-class thugs who ran it. He was afraid of them. While all they could see was the good of the party and their own personal interests, he, on the other hand, was a man of inquiry, a civilian police detective who aspired to discover the truth and catch criminals, whoever they might be.

Franz was drafted into the Gestapo against his will, and he was different from most of the investigators in his approach to questioning suspects. "If I send a suspect to a torture room, he'll confess to anything, even planning the Führer's murder, and he'll be put to death," he taught his underlings. "Everyone will praise my good work. But the potential assassin, the real one, will still be free. Always remember, a bomb that is not neutralized will explode sooner or later."

Like most Germans, he also supported Hitler's rise to power and believed that Hitler "would bring order to the chaos that reigned since the defeat of the Great War." On the other hand, Franz was repulsed by the party's positions on Jews. Indeed, it was the 'good Avram', his mother said, that saved them from misery after his father abandoned them.

Franz had been a toddler then and they had nothing. The 'good Avram' was the one who took care of them, who paid for years of the best kindergartens and elementary schools in Berlin, who bought their clothes and their food. Avram was the one who arranged respectable work for his mother with a Jewish clothes merchant who paid her well. He didn't get drunk and never raised a hand to her; he treated her like a queen. When his wife died young, he invited the mother and son to live with him in his home.

Avram treated Franz like the son he never had. He taught his mother and him about philosophy, art, music, theater. From his position in the Gestapo, Franz witnessed the party's reign of terror inflicted primarily on Jews and convinced his mother and Avram to move to America. He quickly regretted not having left with them. Now it was too late.

However, that afternoon, nothing bothered him. On the contrary, he was feeling deeply relieved because he had succeeded in uncovering and destroying a Jewish underground resistance cell. Although it was a small and marginal group, its existence had greatly disturbed the heads of government and therefore, eliminating it had become an essential mission.

Franz was about to draft the whole story into an orderly report, but a knock on the door interrupted the flow of his thoughts. A frightened clerk mumbled something about a bully who killed two SS officers in the street.

"A Jew?"

"No, but one of the murdered is Gerd Miller."

Franz was suffused with joy. An especially nosy SS officer, a sick sadist, was now out of his way. But it was also clear to him that he would now have to look into who was behind the double murder himself. Indeed, no one in Germany would dare just up and murder a member of the SS, and certainly not a cruel and fearsome thug like Gerd Miller. It must be some network working against the party, he thought.

"Bring him here," said Franz.

The clerk returned with a huge man by his side. His hands were cuffed and chained to the irons around his ankles. Franz looked at him and surmised it would be hard to get the names of his accomplices out of him. He assumed the giant did not murder the two SS men on his own.

Franz signaled to the policemen who entered after them and they sat the large man down on a metal chair screwed to the floor and locked his leg-irons to a ring below it. The man showed no signs of resistance.

Franz studied him for a long time. He learned a lot by looking at people, simply looking, especially before asking questions and before they got defensive. While teaching a course in investigation, he was in the habit of saying to his students, "When a person, any person, starts to speak, he starts to lie. Only a silent person is not lying. Learn as much as you can from the people you are questioning before they utter a single word. The initial observation is a winning tool in the hands of a smart investigator who knows how to use it properly."

Franz knew how to use it better than anyone else. He immediately recognized that the man sitting before him had been beaten up and had not resisted arrest. Apparently, they beat him up good. This fact made Franz happy. It's easier to interrogate someone whose spirit is broken. And still, the giant's calm bothered him. This one behaved like he was threatened by nothing. Mentally retarded? he asked himself and decided to check the matter.

"Release his hands and leave!" Franz barked. You can also learn a lot from the movement of a person's hands. The policemen stared at him anxiously.

"Commander, it was hard to cuff him, we don't know if the commander needs to..."

"It wasn't hard for you," said Franz, his tone calm. "He didn't resist at all, you just laid into him with your billy clubs after you had him restrained."

The policemen nodded and anxiously released the man's hands. "We'll wait outside," one of them said, and they disappeared.

Franz stared long and hard at the man. He was about twenty years old, very tall, maybe just shy of six and a half feet, and broad, his neck as wide as a bull's, with amazingly muscular arms. But despite his size, there was something soft, almost docile, in his behavior.

Franz was surprised to discover that the man looked straight at him, and immediately understood that he was neither mentally impaired nor docile. In his entire life as an investigator, especially since wearing the black uniform of the Gestapo, he had never met a subject who dared to look him in the eye, and certainly not with such clear intensity. Who, in all hell, is this man? It's completely clear he's the leader of some underground. How did I not get any information earlier on a leader of an underground of this size? he thought. Franz made a mental note to admonish his intelligence team for not recognizing a giant like this on the streets of Berlin among the few hundred individuals resistant to the government.

But, before he had a chance to ask him who he was, the man interrupted his thoughts. "You good man, they bad."

Franz, surprised to discover he was being led, rather than the one leading the conversation, asked, "Who is bad? The policemen who brought you in?"

"No, they just no brain. Two I kill, very bad." The giant had a small, soft voice and a heavy foreign accent.

"Wait, you admit you killed them?"

"I force to, but not want to kill," answered the giant, serenely.

Franz stopped, took a deep breath, and took back the reins of the conversation. "Who are you?"

"I Iron Mensch."

"Huh? I want your name, not your nickname."

"Iron Mensch. No other name since small like this." Iron indicated a small space between his thumb and forefinger. "Already then, I strong like iron."

Franz liked to record every word and expression in the conversations he had. As was his habit, he took out a large notebook and an elegant fountain pen and wrote in small, orderly letters on the cover, "Iron Mensch." He was blessed with a phenomenal memory that enabled him to easily recreate entire conversations and interrogations, but the pauses inherent in writing helped him to digest what he was hearing and plan the next steps of the questioning. "Where are you from?"

"Hungaria, no mother, Iron too big, come out and she die. Father beat Iron till he thirteen. Then Iron catch father hand and it break. After, he sell Iron to German circus, circus take Iron to Austria, then here."

Franz was amazed by the flow of words that emerged from Iron's mouth. In the end, it was his personal curiosity rather than the needs of the investigation that determined his next query. "What did you do in the circus as a boy?"

"First, Iron take care of animals, clean, give food. But Iron know how talk to animals, talk with eyes. So he make shows with animals in circus. No hit animals. Just talk with eyes. And make show of great strength."

"Give me an example."

"Iron pull train car with animals inside with teeth, break iron chain, put stage on back with five ladies in pyramid."

Franz grew even more curious. "You can tear the chain binding you to the chair?"

"Yes."

"Why don't you do that and run away? You know what awaits you here?"

Iron shrugged. "Iron kill two bad man. Iron come to police, tell what happen. You good man, why Iron run?"

They hadn't said he turned himself in, thought Franz. These bastard cops ran to boast about how they caught a man who had murdered two SS officers. "Break it. Let's see." Franz pointed at the chain. Iron held two adjacent links in his hands and turned them quickly in opposing directions, back and forth, while pulling. His face reddened but, after a minute, the links separated. He lifted his gaze and looked into Franz' eyes and smiled. "Iron very strong," he said.

Franz hid his surprise and returned to the investigation. "Why did you kill them?"

"They take two baby cats, tie tail of one to tail of other with rope and light rope with fire. Iron try to stop fire with hands and they jump on Iron with sticks and beat Iron. Little cats very scared and scream to mama. Iron want to help, Iron catch bad mens by collar and knock one head to other head and then put out fire."

Iron extended his large hands to display the burns. "After, Iron give baby cats water, find mama cat, and come to station."

"You killed them both with one blow?"

"Yes. Heads no hard like hearts, heads soft."

Franz was quiet for a long minute. "Why did you say I was a good man?"

"Iron father not let Iron grow with mens, only in yard with pigs and chickens and dogs. Iron learn to talk to animals, not with mouth, with eyes. Iron look in animal eyes and that way talk to them. Also mens, inside they have animal. You can see animal only in eyes. Iron not talk good with mens. They laugh at language. But Iron talk to animal inside mens. If animal good, man good."

Again, the investigator succumbed to curiosity, "There are good animals and bad animals?"

"Of course. There is good lion, good horse, and also bad. Rabbit he can make bad. But mens make the most bad."

Can he really read men's souls and detect their truths? If so, I really need someone like him by my side, said Franz to himself. "Can you tell when a man is lying?"

"Mens only lie with mouth, animal inside not lie, never lie. If you talk with animal inside, not with mens, you know if mens lie. Iron also sometimes know what mens think."

"Give me an example, Herr Mensch, what am I thinking about?"

Iron focused his green eyes on Franz' eyes. "You think Iron good man." He was silent a moment and then smiled. "You want Iron close to you, Iron to help you." Again, he was silent, "but Iron not know how help Mr. Policeman," he added sadly.

Yes, dammit, that's a treasure in the hands of a good investigator, thought Franz. He recognizes when someone lies to him. So he eliminated two SS members, but everyone's better off without them. God knows I need a decent guard to protect me from the criminals, and even more from the SS who will, one day, likely discover what I really think of them, and who my adopted father is.

"Do you know how to drive?"

"Yes. Iron drive all truck and car in circus."

Franz's head worked quickly. He thought about how to recruit

Iron into the organization. He knew he was gambling with his life in the event of failure, but he trusted his gut feeling. Still, he owed himself additional proof. "Look at me again, what do you see?"

"You want something, but afraid."

Franz decided to leap into the water. "Look into my eyes and tell me, while those two you killed tied the tails of the cats together, did they say anything?"

Iron looked into the eyes of the investigator, as if trying to learn what they meant. "Mr. Policeman want to save Iron, but why Mr. Policeman afraid? Iron not understand."

"It's not important that you understand, you said I'm a good man, so trust me, that's what's important. Look me in the eyes again and answer. Did any of them say anything about the Führer while burning the cats' tails?"

Iron looked into the eyes of the Gestapo officer and then smiled. "Yes, the tall one he tell the other come burn the Führer's tail and the other he laugh."

"You will remember this answer, Iron?"

"This what is true, sir, this is reason I beat their heads together! Cats not important to Iron."

"If someone with abilities like yours looked into your eyes, what would they say?"

"Iron now learn to lie, but no animal, not even animal of Iron know to lie, Mr. Policeman, sir."

The idea that had sprouted in Franz's mind now ripened into a decision. He would add a section to the report about catching the Jewish underground operating in Berlin. There, he would write that Iron Mensch heard the two conspirators planning to set fire to the Chancellor's residence and he killed them, barehanded, out of loyalty and devotion to the Reich and the party. He understood, of course, that tying them to a Jewish underground was outrageous, but that connection would justify the exaggerated importance the SS leadership gave to the underground. In the conclusion of the report, he would ask that Mr. Mensch be granted the rank of Untersharführer in the Gestapo, and that way he could use him as his personal driver and bodyguard.

Franz called in the policemen, who were shocked to see the broken chains. "Release him, send him to take a shower, get him a uniform in his size and bring him back here to me. Send me the personnel officer."

Franz Schmidt knew he was walking a tightrope. But he believed Iron, and his gut instincts had never been wrong before. He just couldn't have guessed how quickly those instincts would be tested.

# July 1945, Munich

## 1

Dr. Greenberg's room was small and crowded. The space was dominated by a large examination table. At the small desk beside it, Iron and Alexandra sat across from Dr. Greenberg.

"He's a good man, the doctor," Iron whispered in Alexandra's ear. Her heart raced.

"You are the mother of Max Fischer's son?" asked Dr. Greenberg.

Alexandra nodded. She realized this fact aroused a small commotion with the Americans. She expected something good but prepared herself for the worst.

Dr. Greenberg looked at her for a moment. "Mrs. Brecholdt, I want to inform you that, according to the documents we have in hand, Max Fischer's family – his wife, parents, and his son – were murdered in the camps."

The emphasis on the phrase, "his wife" embarrassed Alexandra.

"I...," for a moment, she stammered, but recovered quickly. "I didn't say I was his wife. Max and I acted together in the theater. I had a son by him. I assume that sort of thing happens in America as well, no?"

Her directness made the doctor squirm uncomfortably in his seat.

"I got pregnant by him before the war and, since then, our paths diverged. He didn't know, and apparently doesn't know, about the birth of his son, Thomas."

"Maybe you'd like something stronger to drink?" Dr. Greenberg asked, looking for an excuse to have a drink himself so early in the morning. "It's bourbon, American whisky," he said and without waiting for a response, he presented a generous serving to both Alexandra and Iron. From his first time entering a concentration camp with the US army, he had turned to the bitter-sweet elixir not infrequently.

Iron politely refused, but Alexandra poured the content of the glass directly down her throat and leaned back in her chair.

"So, you say Max has another son who grew up with you."

Alexandra nodded, "Yes, his name is Thomas."

"And, indeed, Max is alive and physically well, relative to the others. This news could greatly assist in his recovery."

"You said physically well?"

"Yes, you see, he is a strong man. Apparently, he ate better than most of the prisoners I've treated. He also received reasonable medical treatment. The commander of the camp made sure to keep him healthy and fit. He's a very intelligent man, and cynical. Very cynical."

"When I saw him about two months ago, he was thin, truly gaunt," said Alexandra.

Dr. Greenberg smiled sadly. "I call that good condition, excellent even. We freed living skeletons from the camps, people who are still having a hard time swallowing solid food."

"I'm sorry, I understand, but at the moment, I'm interested in only one person - Max Fischer. You said he is physically well, so what's the problem?"

"Max underwent a terrible trauma, apparently greater than his ability to withstand. How should I put it simply...?"

"Doctor, stop toying with me, I told you, I went there with him, we both were there." She pointed at herself and Iron. "I know, I saw with my own eyes what happened. Tell me what his problem is today."

Dr. Greenberg's pupils dilated, and he again poured himself bourbon and emptied his glass. "He lost his memory."

"Lost his memory?"

"He remembers nothing."

"What do you mean nothing? There must be things he knows. Memory cannot be erased as if it were written in chalk on a blackboard."

"Honestly ma'am, that is exactly what happened. I don't understand the subject well enough but, according to the testimony I received, one morning he woke up and didn't know where he was or even what his name was. Complete amnesia. It wasn't a result of an external trauma to the head, so I can only assume that Max, somehow, simply shut down his memory to protect himself from the pain. Aside from that, he also sometimes hears in his head, and in his sleep, loud laughter that bothers him.

"May I see him, please?" Iron interrupted the conversation. "Maybe I'll discover something."

The doctor and Alexandra turned to look at him.

"Can you let Iron see Max?" Alexandra asked.

"I don't exactly understand what you want to see," Dr. Greenberg said to Iron.

Iron hesitated. He avoided requests to demonstrate his abilities. They were always met with skepticism by educated people. But the doctor shrugged his shoulders and waited for a response. Iron explained, briefly, his talent for looking into a person's eyes and seeing what he called "the animal within."

"For example, Doctor, you look at ease, but I can read in your eyes that you're in crisis, you feel exhausted and like you've lost your way and the faith you grew up with. You're looking for a single anchor to hold on to. I have no idea what that might be. Now will you let me try to read Max?"

"Good God!" exclaimed Dr. Greenberg. In one glance at his eyes, the giant had surmised his loss of faith in God, the faith he was suckled on in his father's house and lost in the death camps when he comprehended the scale of the catastrophe. He was reminded of how he climbed out of the Jeep and fell to his knees with a cry, "Where were you, our Father in heaven! Where are you?" From that moment on, he lost his religion, his faith, and his soul was without refuge.

"Maybe you really should meet Max," he said. "In any case, I do not have the tools or the knowledge to help him." He turned to Alexandra. "I'll invite him here. I don't think he will remember who you are, please don't try to force anything on him. And please, don't talk to him about his past. You too, Iron. Look at him as you wish, but don't frighten him like you frightened me. We must be careful."

After a short time, they sat across from Max Fischer. Alexandra looked at the man who sat in front of her, and her heart grew heavy. This was not the tall, straight-backed man with the head of thick black hair and sparkling eyes she knew in the theater. Sitting across from her was a man who was stooped, his hair turning white, and his eyes were completely extinguished.

She wiped her damp eyes. He may not have been the man she had been longing for, but she still had to exercise all her restraint not to run to him, to hug and kiss him, to tell him everything. She had so much to tell him. Max looked at her for a long time and was silent. His hands, which she loved so much, rested on his knees. He asked her name.

"Alexandra," she answered, and he repeated it after her, rolling the 'r' in his throat and staring at her with lustful eyes. Clearly, her name and her image were foreign to him.

At the same time, Iron studied Max's eyes but, after only a few minutes, he suddenly dropped his eyes and began to weep.

"Why are you crying, big man?" asked Max. "What, did you have a brother who looked just like me or something?" He turned to the doctor. "Doctor, there are enough cry-babies screaming in my room every night, all night. Why bring me to this crying Hercules?"

"Do you know who Hercules is?" the doctor asked off-hand.

Max shrugged, shook his head no, and asked to return to the yard to continue playing soccer. The doctor nodded. "Before I go," he added and stood up, "did you find a solution to this laugh in my head? No, right? Bye doctor, good-bye dear friends. Alexandra, you said? I'd love to meet you for lunch - in fact, we eat pretty well with the Americans." He smiled at her and left the room.

"What happened, Iron?" Alexandra asked in German. "I've never seen you like this..."

"I saw the great sadness of the animal, a sorrow that screams at the sky. Never in my life, have I seen this kind of sadness in human eyes. I tried to enter it, to approach the beast, to gain its trust and to speak with it, but it was like there was a barrier of death in the way..." Iron avoided looking the others in the eye.

Alexandra translated his words for Dr. Greenberg.

"Apparently, he remembers - remembers and represses," he said. "As I already told you, I have no tools to help him. Maybe you can help me understand him better. Tell me what you saw in the camp."

Alexandra shifted uncomfortably in her chair. "I'd prefer not to talk about it," she said, her voice trembling.

"Then what can I help you with, Mrs. Brecholdt?" he asked.

"According to the notes you have, his family was murdered and he has no living relatives. If that's so, his closest relation is Thomas, my son... our son. Max has a right to meet his son and to know him. He also has the right to know Thomas' mother, the woman who loved him and still... it's his right, Doctor, and mine."

"I'll recommend that he is released to your care, but he will have to approve the request. Please come back tomorrow and we'll take it from there."

## 2

Iron and Alexandra drove in silence through the wreckage of buildings and piles of bricks and debris.

It was Alexandra who broke the silence.

"Max lost everything dear to him, he... maybe he's better off without his memory."

"It's true he put a wall up between himself and his suffering, but he is suffering. I have never seen such terrible suffering in a person's eyes before. He is completely alone, and he can't share his suffering with anyone. His animal does not know how to speak, but it remembers everything and is hurting. The person, who does know how to speak, remembers nothing and, therefore, cannot speak about it. How long do you think an animal is able to withstand that kind of pain, alone, before it is torn apart? I don't know what this doctor knows or doesn't know, but he is a good man who wants to help. Listen to his advice. You love Max, you truly love him. Which is why I think you have only one choice, and you know what it is."

"I've never heard such a long monologue from you before. Thank you. You've helped me." Alexandra kissed his cheek, set a time to meet the next morning, and went up to her apartment where her son was waiting for her.

# Berlin, 1918

## 1

"The wind is carrying the gas back towards us! Run, run! Gas! Run!"

The father's screams woke Alexandra. Nightmares again disturbed his sleep. She covered her head with a pillow, but she still heard her mother rush to him, calm him with her voice, soft like a hug. After several minutes, the yelling turned to weeping, and then quieted. Her father fell asleep. Pretty quickly this time, she thought. Sometimes the process took hours. Sometimes the nightmares turned into outbursts of rage that ended with broken furniture. Less frequently, they also turned violent, and her mother hid the bruises in the morning. No matter how hard she tried, Alexandra could not fall back to sleep.

She missed her father, the father she had before he was drafted into the Great War, before he wore a pressed uniform and held a shiny gun and bayonet. She felt like that chapter was part of another world, in a life that wasn't hers, but she remembered that day so well, the warm summer day when she traveled with her father and mother to the train. She had been so proud of her father, the soldier, in the way only a six-year-old girl can be.

On the train platform, a large clock displayed the date and hour. August 23, 1916, 09:33. He kissed her, promised he would return from France and bring her lots of presents. She cried and he asked her to stop, to take care of her mother, and read the books he had left for her. "There's a whole beautiful world in books, remember that" he said. He kissed her mother and boarded the train.

She didn't cry anymore. She read from the books he left and from the new books that arrived at their home – and waited for him. She waited for two years. Two years, two months, and one day. She added the count to the prayer she recited each night until he returned.

Alexandra recalled precisely the day hundreds of wounded, bandaged, and disabled men stepped off the train. She was so frightened. "Dear Jesus," she whispered and crossed her fingers, "make him come home healthy and whole." And she immediately heard her mother's call, "Here's Father."

She recognized him immediately. Just like she remembered, handsome and tall and with no injuries at all. Her body shook with joy, and she burst forward, pushing between all the people. "Papa" was the only word she was able to get out of her mouth after she ran into his arms and hugged and kissed him over and over. "Papa, Papa…."

"Look at you, my girl," he said. "I said goodbye to a little girl, and here is a beautiful young lady welcoming me!" She blushed, and just then, her mother arrived. Her father just stared at her and kissed her on the cheek.

She remembered that he fell asleep in the car on the way home, and asked her mother if he wasn't happy to see them. Her mother answered that he was just tired. "We are very lucky," she said.

Yes, they were lucky. Returning to their home was a man strongly resembling the father and husband who left them. But his laughing eyes, full of goodness, now raced non-stop, as if they were searching for something that wasn't there. His wonderful voice, a voice she yearned for every time she took a book in hand, had become tense and moody. By the next day, Alexandra had already discovered that every little thing made him angry.

And there were also the nights. The nights without quiet, the nightmares in which he screamed, and from which he woke drenched in cold sweat. "Give him time," her mother said, "Papa will heal. A little time and a lot of love, that's all he needs."

Through the years that followed, Alexandra tried to believe her. Life with her father oscillated between outbursts of anger, depression, and crisis, and those better days when the best of fathers could again be found; he sat next to her, reading books and plays, explaining and listening. Sometimes he worked hard on Shakespearean language, or on the meaning hidden between the lines; sometimes he asked her to read aloud to him and act out the role of the women in the play. Those good days kept a flicker of hope alive in her heart.

## 2

As a child, as soon as she learned to read and write, her father would take her to the theater with him. She loved the plays and would watch with total concentration, catching sentences, and reviewing them on their way home.

"When I grow up, I will be a theater actress," she declared to her father, who could not contain his smile.

Upon the father's departure for the front, the mother seeded her own passion in her despondent daughter. She taught her to read sheet music, play the piano, and sing in a clear voice. When Alexandra turned eight, her mother took her to concerts and plays as often as was possible during wartime. Although Alexandra loved the theater very much, the plays awakened a terrible longing for her father and, therefore, she preferred the musical evenings.

Indeed, once her father returned from the war, on the days when his spirits were quiet, they returned to the theater. At the end of the play, they would sit together for long hours analyzing every character in the play, their motivations, and desires. And she argued with him, defending her opinions like a teenager. When they agreed on the nature of the characters, father and daughter would perform bits from the play for her mother, who would applaud enthusiastically and always demanded an encore.

When she was old enough and knew the plays of Shakespeare inside-out, she was drawn to the dark figure of Othello, the black-skinned war hero, the generous warrior. He, who despite his fierce love for his young wife, Desdemona, strangled her to death in a fit of jealousy. She loved Othello and also hated him. Iago, the villain in the play who incited Othello to think his spouse had betrayed his trust, she despised.

"How could a loving man strangle his wife to death?" she asked her father. "The Evil Spirit entered him. He wasn't himself," he tried to explain the inexplicable. Alexandra, who had seen the Evil Spirit enter her father's body, shrugged her shoulders, and picked up the book and again tried to understand.

"It can't be that jealousy is stronger than love," she said upon completing her reading. Her father shrugged his shoulders. "You tell that to Mr. Shakespeare," he said.

"But what do you think, Papa?"

"I want to believe that you are mostly right," he answered, "but sometimes there are extraordinary circumstances." She shivered as if someone had opened a window in the middle of winter. Maybe she sensed, without even noticing, that a similar triangle connecting a man, a woman, and Satan in the figure of a man, would become the story of her life.

# July 1945, Munich

## 1

Iron turned the nose of the Mercedes towards the rear entrance of the building and his apartment, one floor below Alexandra's. Because of the chaos in the streets of Munich, she wanted him as close as possible.

His was a big apartment with high ceilings and wood-paneled walls. However, the heavy furniture left behind by the previous owners, and the fact that Iron rarely opened the blinds, made it look terribly crowded and over-stuffed. But, at that moment, Iron was not concerned with the design of his apartment. He was only interested in the beautiful Gypsy girl with eyes like a deer – large and brown - who waited for him there.

Iron had saved her two days earlier when he lifted a wooden beam that had fallen on her with the collapse of a building. Along with the thousands of other women left alone in the cities of Germany, she searched the ruins for any treasure that she could trade for necessities on the black market. Iron heaved the beam off her body and carried her in his arms from the rubble. He made sure she was not injured and saw in her eyes despair and fear diluted with goodness and longing. "I'll take you to your home," he said.

"I have no home, big guy, just put me down here on the side of the road."

Iron asked her permission to take her to his house, and she nodded. He carried her the whole way, and when they arrived, he washed her and laid her down in his bed.

"Thank you, I am Aishé," she whispered and fell asleep before he said his name.

Iron immediately went to the black market and got her clothes. They were waiting for her the next morning. After many days in which no food had reached her lips, she feasted to her heart's content on a satisfying breakfast. When she finished, she asked his name and offered him her body. Iron smiled and kissed her on the forehead. He showed her where the food was kept and went out about his day.

He knew he would find her at home when he returned. And indeed, at the entrance to the building, he could already smell the cooking and baking. He found her in the kitchen, juggling between the pots situated on the kerosene burners.

"Don't know watcha like to eat. So, I made vegetable soup and stew from the meat and lentils you left, and I baked fresh bread. But I couldn't find anything hot. How can a big man like you live without hot pepper?"

"I like to eat everything and a lot of it, spicy too." Iron smiled, "But first things first. Now we'll eat. Then we'll talk about whatever you want." Iron didn't know that with these words he made his mark on the girl's heart and she would be his forever.

## 2

Equipped with the letter that Dr. Greenberg wrote for her, Alexandra sat before the American administrative officer.

"I understand you're the mother of Max Fischer's son, that you are aware of his condition and, according to Dr. Greenberg's professional opinion, you will take care of him in a suitable fashion. Please fill out this form and sign it."

Alexandra worried that the process itself would take weeks but, upon signing the document releasing the Americans of all responsibility for the physical and mental condition of Max Fischer, Max himself entered the room so he could be asked for his consent.

The Americans were very happy for someone to take one more survivor off their hands, a fact that easily prevailed over the bureaucracy.

"The lady would like to take you home to her house, she says she has a surprise for you. Do you agree to go live with her?"

Max looked at Alexandra and answered with a wide smile. "Miss Brecholdt, maybe no one has told you this, but you are a painfully beautiful woman. Of the little I've heard from you, you are also smart, assertive, and you also appear to be wealthy. What would you want of me? I'm a Jew, broken, with no memory, desire, or ambition. Chased by laughter that wakes me up at night. And I'm an obsessive jokester… believe me, for your own good, whatever reason you're looking for a Jew, there are more interesting ones than me, right here in the camp. Dr. Greenberg, for example, he's a bachelor."

During the previous long, sleepless night, Alexandra imagined a slew of possible responses from Max and how she would answer them. But she had not expected a refusal. She tried to digest his words.

"Alex, call me Alex," she said.

"Okay, Alex. Wait a minute… you said, Alex?"

"A Jewish friend used to call me that," she said.

Max restrained himself from spitting the terrible joke that came to mind about blue-eyed women attracted to Jewish men with long noses. "Look, miss, uh, Alex, I'd be happy to work for you in any capacity you'd like, but I'm no *groisse metziya*, really not a catch at all. It's important to me that I give you the whole picture, so you won't be disappointed."

Alexandra smiled. She'd heard these Yiddish words from his lips more than once. "*Die bist.*" She answered him quickly in the language he had used and repeated the words with a German intonation. "You are so." She hoped that as they got their distance from the camp, when she brought him into her home and to their son, he would remember her. She impatiently waited the moment her family would be united, and she would rejoice.

She had no idea how many times she would be on the verge of breaking.

Sometimes, not knowing is a blessing.

## 3

They drove without exchanging a word. Max looked around him. For the first time, he saw the extent of the damage after the war. Battered roads and demolished buildings on every corner, piles upon piles of rubble that had once been extravagant homes. In the remnants of one of the buildings he could make out hungry Germans fighting over a piece of bread, or over some pathetic object they looted, as if it were a sparkling diamond.

He watched and remained silent, embarrassed by the satisfaction he felt from how pathetic the residents of Munich had become. The woman sitting next to him was indeed beautiful. He knew that, in another world, he certainly would have tried to get close to her. But what he didn't know was what motivated her to take him in, and therefore, he was suspicious of her.

The man driving the car added to his misgivings. Iron? What kind of name is that? Had he made a mistake by giving up the relative safety provided by the Americans? "Know from where you came and to where you are going," the Mishnaic line from the *Ethics of the Fathers*, rang in his ear, a line he heard on the way to bury one of his few friends. Max knew only that he had come from a death camp. And he had no idea where he was going.

# April 1945,
## Kaufering Concentration Camp, Bavaria

### 1

A crazy laugh woke him from his sleep. His mouth was dry, and his temples pounded. When he sat up awake, aside from the disturbing laugh, he heard sawing snores, strangled screams, and crying. He hadn't known there were so many kinds of crying: whimpered, strangled, bitter, screaming, silent. "Stop laughing already, you're driving me crazy!" he yelled.

"So, you're finally awake, I was afraid it would never happen. You've haven't moved a finger in two days. Max, are you okay?"

He looked over at two figures who sat up in their bunks. They were so thin, they were nearly transparent.

"We were worried about you," said one of them.

Someone lit a candle. Max closed his eyes, rubbed them with his fists, sat up, and opened them. Despair, hunger, and want came at him from every direction... He was in a long, dark, foul-smelling barracks, crammed with the human skeletons dressed in rags who crowded one right next to the other into a double layer of bunks. He started to recognize the sources of the snoring, the sighs, the crying, but he could not find who was responsible for the laughter. No matter which direction he turned his head, it seemed the laugh came from there. He turned to the figure standing before him. "Were you talking to me?"

"Yes."

"Who is Max?"

"You."

"Me? Since when?"

"Maybe you don't remember, maybe because of what happened…," said the skeleton.

"It doesn't matter now, just ask the mad person who's laughing to stop. My head is exploding…"

The two figures nodded to one another in understanding.

"Max, do you remember me? Do you know where you are? I'm Motl, the Pole."

"You certainly sound Polish, but who are you, and why am I supposed to remember you?" He looked for a moment at his hand, at his sleeve, and then at his tattered shirt and pants. "I'm covered in blood!" he yelled. "Did I murder someone? Am I in prison?"

The Pole looked at him with compassion. "One could say that, but you didn't murder anyone – on the contrary."

The skeletal one held Motl's arm and hinted with his eyes – go slowly. Motl nodded and kept quiet.

"On the contrary? Someone murdered me? I'm in hell?"

"No and yes, they haven't murdered you yet, but you are in hell. In essence, we all are."

Motl wet a piece of dry bread and gave it to Max.

Max chewed on the damp bread absent-mindedly, and suddenly it became clear to him that he had no idea who he was, where he was, and why it was that he was trying to remember something and kept getting stuck in a dark chasm.

"Is there anything other than this bread to eat here?" he asked.

"Breakfast is soon, there will also be a little soup."

"Where does one piss here? I'm dying to pee…"

"There," Motl pointed, "but come back quickly, inspection is soon."

Max went and then returned to his bunk, closed his eyes, and allowed the darkness to return and take control of his senses.

## 2

And again, he was awakened by the laughter. He covered his head with the rags that served as his blanket, but the laugh grew stronger. He sat up, and his gaze fell upon the skeleton man. "Who are you?" he asked.

"Rolf. You know me."

"Do you know who's laughing?"

"It's… in your head. You better get up quickly, we're going out."

Max stood up and started to plod forward while trying to figure out how the laughter followed him, sometimes from behind and sometimes from ahead. But Rolf and Motl the Pole prodded him. "Come, come, you can't be late. Come with us, act like us. Until now, you helped us survive, now we'll help you."

"How did I help you? How am I even capable of helping anyone? Please help me figure out who I am."

"Slowly, slowly," said Motl. "But first we stay alive and staying alive means heading out now to be on time for roll call, which means food. You're lucky they let you sleep for two days without killing you…"

Max tried to get more details, but he came up against a wall in the shape of purpose. The people in the barracks rushed outside into the cold of not-yet-spring. Before long, Max would understand why they hurried.

While they stood at attention, they heard shooting from the direction of the barracks. Max tried to talk to those standing next to him, but their eyes, frozen straight ahead, shut him up immediately. An SS officer signaled to several men who ran to the barracks and came out dragging the bodies of those who had been shot. These were tossed into a cart and taken away. It all happened so quickly. Only minutes later, smoke rose from the chimney with the smell of burnt flesh.

"More food for you," said the German soldier disdainfully. His gaze fell on Max. "Look here, Sleeping Beauty has awoken and is gracing us with his presence, the honorable Mr. Theater Actor himself. The Commandant will be happy to hear you're back to yourself." And then he clapped his hands and yelled, "Come on, rats!"

Everyone fell on the plates piled off to the side, they grabbed slices of moldy bread and a mug of warm water with left-over vegetables. Max was so stunned he was left without even a crumb.

"Next time, move faster and push, you're in better physical condition than the rest of us, use your elbows. In the meantime, eat mine." The Pole gave Max a slice of bread and half a cup of soup. Max was starving and didn't resist. After a few minutes, the men were divided into two groups. The large group was taken in trucks to an adjacent factory, and the second group comprised of Max, the Pole, Rolf, and two other Jews, were taken to the camp archives. Their job was to remove the binders that were to be burned.

At noon, a siren went off. The German soldiers rushed to the anti-aircraft canons positioned around the camp, and in the archive, a single guard was left alone.

"We can run away! There's only one guard!" Max exclaimed to Rolf who was working next to him.

"Someone is bombing the Germans," said Rolf. "It's probably the

English. It's almost over, no one wants to die now, moments before liberation. We must survive to tell. Look how they're burning all the evidence so no one will know what happened here, so they won't hear about the forced labor, the systemized murder, the starvation, the experiments they conducted here on living people…" Rolf noticed the guard getting closer and stopped talking.

That night, Rolf told Max details about his past.

"Your name is Max Fischer. You are one of the biggest theater actors in Germany…"

"I'm a clown," Max interrupted him. Rolf flinched.

"Why would you say that?"

"I don't know… I'm not a clown?"

"You were for a short time, Max. Today, we're all clowns in this horrible theater of the absurd. But I was a historian, and you were an actor, primarily a classical, Shakespearean actor."

Max looked at him in disbelief. The three continued to burn documents over the coming days and, at night, Rolf would tell him about his past as an actor, about the history of the new Germany and about the war. About himself, he said he was a professor of history and German culture at the University of Heidelberg but, in 1935 with the passage of the race laws, he was fired from his position, and all his academic work went up in flames. Then he was forced to divorce his German wife.

"I barely made a living from temporary work and from teaching in a school for our children," he said. "In 1942, the Nazis discovered that I was seeing my wife. I have no idea what they did to her, but me, they threw here. You were already an old-timer when I arrived. An old-timer and well-respected because you helped everyone."

"Do you know when I got here?" Max asked.

"No, I only know that you've been here the longest. The doctor, who got here before you, died of tuberculosis a year ago. As a matter of principal and wisdom, you didn't want to talk about the life you had before you arrived here, or to remember it. 'Life is what happens here and now,' you said. 'If we think about the past, about what we lost, we will also lose the future.'"

"I said that? Are you sure?"

"Yes. And many of those who are still here survived because you insisted on it."

Max was eager to discover more about his past and continued his nightly conversations with Rolf. But they didn't get him any closer to understanding why his memory had abandoned him.

A few days later, in the dead of night, Rolf woke Max and invited him to join a conversation with the Pole and the two Jews who worked alongside them, burning the archives.

"In talking to you," said Rolf, "I remembered the fact that I am a historian. We are criminals, we are helping the Germans burn the history of the camp! Up until now, we've been burning binders from years ago, but today I saw that we've reached more recent years when tens of thousands of people were murdered. There is careful documentation, names, dates, the method of death. We must hide the binders to preserve the evidence, so no one will be able to say it didn't happen!" He looked at his friends, who nodded. "Tomorrow morning, we will return some of the binders to the cabinets that have already been emptied. We must do it for ourselves, for history, for our dead brothers. But it's important that you all know, if the Germans catch us, we're…"

Rolf didn't complete the sentence, and no one asked him what he was going to say.

The next day, right under the guards' noses, the group began to hide binders that documented the names of the murdered. During the last hour of the fourth day of this mission, Rolf was caught looking through one of the binders. The German guard slammed him in the head with the butt of his gun, dragged him to the courtyard and shot him. "Don't you dare stop working!" he yelled and sent the Pole to throw Rolf's body in the crematorium.

The Pole did so with tears in his eyes and the mourner's *kaddish* mumbled on his lips, "*Yisgadol vyishsabach, shmei rabaw...*"

Upon returning to the barracks, the Pole told Max he would continue the pursuit to save the documents.

"You stop, I'll continue," said Max. "I don't remember anything and won't be able to tell them what happened here. You must live so you can tell, and we're already hearing the canons of the liberators, they're close..."

"They won't believe this actually happened if we don't present documentation, I will continue."

That night, one of them took out a violin and quietly played a traditional Passover melody. "According to my calculations, tonight's the first night of Passover," he whispered. Someone awoke from his sleep and yelled, "You want us to celebrate our freedom?! Go back to sleep!" Max welcomed the sounds of the violin which overpowered the mad laugh that echoed in his head.

Later that night, they heard a commotion outside the barracks. Shooting, cars, commands, and shouting. No one dared go outside to see what was happening.

When they went outside for the morning line-up, they discovered that, aside from the bodies of several of those who apparently tried to escape under the cover of the commotion and several dead soldiers, the camp was empty. The large iron gate at the entrance was wide open.

## 3

Just as a bird raised in a cage is afraid to fly through its open door, the frightened prisoners did not dare approach the open gate. A handful sought food in the camp offices, in the warehouses, in the kitchens, in the officers' dormitories, and in the garbage pails. However, the food stores, like the rest of the camp, were completely empty. The Germans had burned everything that was left behind.

Only Max, whose memories of the camp had shrunk to only a few days and didn't remember anything about his life in the cage, tried to convince them to look for the liberating forces – but he did not have much success.

They did not have to wait long. In the distance, they heard the rumbling of approaching vehicles. "The Germans are returning!" the cry went up, and all the prisoners flew in a tumult, each to his barracks and each to his bunk. Only Max remained outside, trembling with cold and excitement, the hysterical laugh in his head nearly extinguished by the fever that gripped him.

And thus, when three Jeeps flying American flags entered the camp gates, he stood before them alone, thin as a skeleton, dressed in rags, a blue cloth hat perched on his head and waved. "Welcome!" Max called in German. "Where are you coming from?" The Americans, their weapons in hand, ready for any trap, answered in English, "We are soldiers of the US army. Where is the commander of this camp?"

"Welcome," answered Max in fluent English, "We've been waiting for you... we think the commander fled..."

"It's the Americans, they're here!" he roared, not realizing the strength of his call. Prisoners emerged from every hole – Russians, Gypsies, the mentally disabled, members of the resistance, but mostly, Jews. At first, they peeked out in trepidation, as if they were carefully sniffing the outside air, and slowly, the deluge began. Prisoners surged towards the American Jeeps, cried, yelled, kissed the vehicles, touched the uniforms of the soldiers, and mostly begged for food.

The horror was in full display before the young soldiers who took out their battle rations, opened cans of food, and passed out cigarettes. Some of them cried bitterly. "Eagle, this is Three," the communication officer called with emotion through his radio. "We've reached a prison camp. Send doctors and food. Over."

"Three, from Eagle, the doctors recommend not giving the prisoners solid food, I repeat, do not give solid food, it's dangerous for their health. A medical division is heading out in your direction in three minutes. Send an exact location. Over."

And indeed, the prisoners who ate from the canned meat had already thrown their guts up.

Max volunteered to assist with translating from German to English and vice-versa. The Americans kicked into gear and began functioning efficiently throughout the camp. The prisoners received light food and drink, and the doctors circulated among them and provided medical treatment.

Late that night, they turned out the lights and, for the first time, the prisoners were granted a night free of guards, floodlights, and the barking of attack dogs. But not one among them had a night free of nightmares. Most would not enjoy a single quiet night for the rest of their lives.

Many of the American officers and soldiers cried like children when they entered the crematoriums and found piles of shoes, hats, and gold teeth. Only the next morning did Max find the Pole and stick close to him. Together, they delivered to the Americans the binders they succeeded in saving. For the German Jew, Professor Rolf Bauer, as well as many other Jews killed just days before the camps were liberated, it was too late.

# 4

"Your general condition is not bad," the young American medical officer, Dr. Greenberg, said to Max who sat across from him. "You suffered from hunger less than most, you have no significant bruises. But you suffer from amnesia, the loss of your memory, the reason for which is unclear. The laughter you hear may be connected to the amnesia. I'm not entirely sure and, for now, I don't know how to treat it. We will keep you here under our care for as long as we can and try to get information regarding how best to treat you."

The Jewish doctor was reminded again of the testimony of Motl and his friends. Max was the one who saved their lives, they said. He was the one who smuggled food and medicine. "He also made us laugh, and kept our morale up," they added. Maybe it's better for him not to remember, he said to himself. After all, he must have erased his memory, himself, because he didn't want to remember.

Dr. Greenberg's thoughts wandered to Max's only friend, Motl, who lay like a stone in his bed. He didn't tell Max that his friend could barely digest any food, that he was suffering from severe pneumonia and apparently, his days were numbered. He could not understand how, in his condition, Motl had managed to save the documents from destruction by the Nazis.

For a moment, only for a moment, the doctor called for God's help, but then was immediately filled with rage. "God is dead," he whispered to himself.

"Doctor, did you say something?" Max asked.

"Sorry, I was reminded of my father, who still lays *tefillin* and prays *shacharis* every morning. He was lucky he wasn't born here in Germany. Where were we?"

"You said…" Max imitated the doctor's Brooklyn accent, "that in general my condition is good, but I have amnesia and you want to leave me here for observation. What am I, a clown in this nightmarish circus of yours? Do you talk about me with your friends at night?"

"I'm sorry, I… didn't know you felt that way, and of course, I don't speak to anyone about your condition…"

"I'm sorry, Dr. Greenberg, I'm the one who should apologize. I don't know what demon took control of my head."

"In the documents we found, it says you had a wife by the name of Berta and a son named David. Try to remember them."

"I don't remember any Berta," said Max, "And I don't know who David is, I don't know what you want from me." His voice grew to a scream. "Leave me alone, okay? Leave me be!" Max's eyes rolled back in his head, and he began to foam at the mouth.

"A syringe of valium, fast!" Dr. Greenberg called to the nurse that sat outside the room, but with the same speed at which Max exploded, he also calmed down and began to sob.

The nurse entered the room and took Max to the room he shared with other survivors. He lay down in his bed made up with white sheets.

## 5

"Max, get up! Get up fast!" Max heard the voice of Dr. Greenberg.

"What? What happened?"

"Your friend, Motl Epstein is burning with fever, and he asked us to bring you to him quickly."

Max jumped to his feet, "I didn't even know his last name was Epstein," he said.

Dr. Greenberg strode towards the clinic and Max hurried after him.

"I'm here Motl," Max said. Motl, his face dripping with sweat, turned to him. "I came, it's Max Fischer."

"Yes, I… am so sorry about what happened. You didn't deserve it." He signaled for Max to come closer.

"I want to ask you for something," he whispered. "I left a wife in Lodz," he whispered. "A non-Jewish wife. We had a son. Her name is Marta, Marta Berlinska. The boy was called… I'm not sure what he was called, I didn't know him. Find them, help them if you can, tell the boy about his father. Give him this note…" He pushed a wrinkled page into Max's hand.

"Of course, I'll help them, but you're not going anywhere."

Motl coughed and spat blood. His voice was a cracked whisper. "You were the best of all of us, you were the only…"

And he was silent. His eyes remained open. Max felt a hand rest on his shoulder. He turned to Dr. Greenberg, questioning.

"Yes, he's not suffering anymore."

"And what will happen to me? Now, no one is left…"

Max left the room. He did not forget the last request of the man who was his support and friend.

Eventually, when a gap opened in the Iron Curtain that allowed him to travel to Poland, he located the wife and son of Motl the Pole. He met with them and stayed in their home in a village near Lodz. Piotr, Motl's son, grew into a tall young man and his smile reminded Max of his father's smile – the one time he saw his father smile. Max gave him the note his father wrote, and Piotr read it with a smile. "You knew my father? What kind of man was he?" he asked in Polish, which his mother translated into broken German. To the boy, Max described a heroic man who fought the Germans until his last breath. To Marta, he gave a not insignificant amount of money. "Motl asked me to give you this."

"Thank you," she said, "I knew he wouldn't forget me."

# July 1945, Munich

## 1

Max, who for several short months had been the uncrowned king of the survivors at the American rehabilitation camp, found himself sitting in a car with a beautiful woman and a huge man with penetrating eyes.

"May I ask, honorable folk, if it wouldn't be too difficult for you to answer, where are we going?"

"I'm sorry," Alexandra answered empathically, "I'm just so excited…"

"Your response doesn't exactly answer my question," Max chuckled.

"Yes, oh, we're going home to my place. I have a young son, seven-years-old, whom I want you to meet. I've arranged for you to have your own living quarters, with complete privacy."

"Mmm… and… what is expected of me? Surely, they are no gifts without some strings attached…" Max's cynicism became genuine curiosity.

"Maybe we'll begin with conversations about literature, theater, that sort of thing…"

"Mrs. ehh… my apologies, Alex, I know where you're trying to lead me, they told me I was a preeminent actor, but I am no longer that actor. I don't remember how to act. A small problem, no? Wait, did they tell you the reason for my amnesia? Or is it a state secret for you, too?"

Alexandra remained silent. She was afraid the tone of her voice would give her away. Iron looked at Max's eyes through the rear-view mirror. He saw hope. Max's animal was attracted to the woman and wanted to burst out into the world or, he thought with satisfaction, as the doctor had said, the unconscious wanted to break into the conscious.

Alexandra's determination was apparent in her eyes, but there was also deep worry. Iron knew that, with the assistance of his extraordinary senses, he would be able to help her, to tell her when the animal was crawling out of its den, and when it was digging in.

## 2

The first night in his new home was jammed with the mad laugh he heard in his head, images of the camp that rose in his nightmares, and the sound of an explosion accompanied by a feeling of falling into an infinite black hole. Max woke up at six in the morning, covered in cold sweat, and immediately went into the bathroom.

The previous day, Alexandra had led him to a large, luxurious apartment and put two keys in his hand. One was to the front door, and one was for a wing with a large bedroom, a walk-in closet and dressing room, and a bathroom. In the closet, he found clothes in his size: underwear and socks, shirts, pants, suits and ties, shoes, boots, a winter coat, and a raincoat. In the living room there were books, hundreds of books, arranged on the bookshelves by subject.

And as if that weren't enough, Alexandra gave him a sum of money, two-weeks of living expenses, she said. All that she asked was that he come to meals at seven in the morning and seven in the evening, after which they would talk over a cup of coffee or tea for the length of an hour. "Lunch," she said, "you're welcome to eat whenever you wish. At home, or out in the city."

The night before, he found a toothbrush and a refreshing, American, mint-flavored toothpaste waiting for him in the bathroom. There was also shaving cream, a razor, and a leather strap on which to sharpen it.

Max looked at the face reflected in the mirror. He didn't exactly recognize the person before him. "Who are you?" he asked. He was astounded by his good luck which led him from a death camp to the American rehabilitation camp and, from there, to this house, to the woman who any man in the world would want to be near.

Max lathered the shaving soap in its dish and spread the white cream on his face. And, just as it had in the mirror the Americans had provided him, the white painted face again sparked his imagination. A clown, he thought. I am a clown.

It's reasonable to assume that not a one of you, dear readers, has ever experienced the extraordinary situation in which Max found himself. Yet, if you could imagine you were in his place, wouldn't you be suspicious of the lady's intentions? Wouldn't you be afraid of her? Of her huge, strange bodyguard? Wouldn't you wonder about the source of her wealth in a city where most people were fighting over a loaf of bread?

Max began to shave his face. He was indeed frightened by the unknown. Maybe the lady was interested in his performing unspeakable acts for her? He looked at his clean-shaven face, washed off the rest of the soap and dried his face with a towel. And, again, he heard the rolling laughter in his head. He had nothing to lose. With the death of Motl, he didn't know a single soul on the face of the earth who he could call a friend. His cohorts had been a handful of survivors from the camp. No one would look for him. And so, he decided that whoever this woman may be, and whatever her intentions were, he would stay in her home and whatever would be, would be.

He chose a pair of light-colored cotton pants and a dark, casual shirt. Another glance in the mirror confirmed that he was suitably dressed to honor the woman with whom he would be eating breakfast. When had he ever wanted or cared about this kind of thing before? He didn't remember. "And still, I have desires..." he whispered to the mirror.

In the dining room, he met the housekeeper who toiled over coffee and eggs. Aside from her, there was no one.

"Hello, my name is Max. Are we alone today?" he asked.

"Sir arrived early. Soon, the prince and lady come," she answered him with a local Bavarian dialect he barely understood. The prince, he thought. And just then Thomas burst into the dining room on a tricycle, his mother right behind him.

"Good morning," the boy called happily and stared at Max. "Are you the guest Mama promised?"

"I don't know what Mama promised, but I am Max, and I'm pleased to meet you."

"I'm Thomas. Do you know what present I got from Uncle Iron?"

"The handsome shirt?"

"No, Mother buys my shirts. He bought me a real bicycle! And he promised that today he'll teach me to ride it."

Max picked up a broom that was in the kitchen and rode over to the boy on it. "I don't need a bicycle; I have a broom. No need for a bicycle; I've got a broom!" Max cried. The boy burst out laughing.

"I see you don't need me to introduce you," Alexandra joined in with her son's laughter. Max looked her over. She wore a flowered dress that almost reached her knees, and her face was flushed. "Good morning," he said and returned the broom to its place.

Alexandra was about to answer him, but Thomas raced towards her on the tricycle grabbing her attention. She pet the boy's blond head while asking Max about his first night in the house. "The smell of eggs fried in butter makes it impossible for me to answer you at the moment," he answered her.

Alexandra smiled and sat down at the table. The eggs came quickly, and then kettles of coffee and tea, slices of toast, cheese, and two kinds of jam - cherry and pear.

"I make the jams myself," the housekeeper said proudly.

Thomas joined them and gobbled down his breakfast ravenously. Max also ate heartily. Alexandra tasted from this and that, but mostly her eyes held both her dear ones. Does he know this is his son? Will he look in his eyes and see his reflection?"

"Soon I'll go over Iron's day with him," she said. "I'll try to involve you in his work, as I'll be busy all morning. You know nothing about me; I'm building soup kitchens and organizations to feed all the hungry people – mostly women - who are filling the streets…"

Iron entered the room with a wide smile on his face.

"It looks like you had a good night," Alexandra said. "Someone I know?"

Iron smiled and kissed her cheek. Thomas ran to him, and he tossed him in the air, hugged him to his chest, and said hello to Max. Afterwards, he also kissed the housekeeper on the cheek who blushed like a girl.

"No, you haven't met her yet," he said. "But you will love her. There's something independent about her, unbridled. Like you."

Alexandra looked at him, curious. She had never heard him speak more than a word or two about someone he had spent the night with.

"Invite her to dinner?"

"It's still too early for that, but I hope you'll meet soon."

"You're going to take me to ride on the bicycle outside, right?" asked Thomas.

"I'm not sure, buddy," said Iron, "Maybe this afternoon."

"But Uncle Iron, you promised you'd take me, you didn't promise maybe..."

"You're right. No maybes."

"Would you like to go with Iron on his morning rounds?" Alexandra asked Max. "He's responsible for my properties and helps me collect rent from the tenants and shopkeepers."

Max was glad to go out and wander the city, and to accompany a man the likes of whom he had never known. "The properties," as Alexandra called them, were dozens of apartments and shops throughout the city. Some were completely ruined; some were in various stages of renovation and construction and others were occupied.

Despite his pleasant manner, Max realized that most of the tenants were wary of Iron. Iron looked into the eyes of those who had a host of excuses not to pay and sometimes agreed to put off the payments, sometimes reduced the payments, and sometimes – if he determined they were trying to cheat – he demanded immediate payment.

His appreciation of Iron grew when, in one of the stores, the young tenant threatened him with an iron rod. Iron caught his arm, pulled the rod out of the tenant's hand, held it by both ends and pressed. To Max's wonder and the obvious trepidation of the tenant, the rod surrendered to Iron's muscles and bent. Iron tossed the bar aside and looked at the tenant. "The days of violence in Germany are over," he said quietly. "I'll give you two weeks grace because I sense your distress."

"As strong as you are, that's how gentle you are," Max said when he returned to the car.

Iron looked at Max and smiled. "The strength allows me not to be afraid, and he who isn't afraid, or hungry – doesn't attack. Every animal knows that. But I see that you are also not afraid. You're not afraid of anything."

"What could someone with no memory be afraid of, without benefit of life experience to teach him to be wary or careful… There are advantages to my situation."

Iron looked at him for a long moment, and said quietly, "And maybe someone who has already seen the worst of all has nothing to fear." He was pleased to discover in Max's dead eyes a spark of wonder, as if a crack appeared in the armor that enveloped him. But Max immediately shrugged and, just in a blink of an eye, the opacity had returned to his eyes. Iron didn't know that in that moment a sickening laugh rolled in Max's head.

In the early afternoon, the two returned to Alexandra's house. "I promised Thomas that I would teach him to ride a two-wheeler. We'll continue working tomorrow."

Iron turned to his apartment. To his surprise, Aishé had disappeared without even a note, and the money he had left on the table disappeared with her. From the time he was a boy, he was familiar with life's disappointments. He knew why the girl had been tempted by the easy money. His disappointment came from not reading her correctly.

He took off his clothes and got into the shower. There, under the stream of chilly water that washed over him, he remembered her and burst into tears. Of all the women he had known, she was the first he had wanted to stay. And yet, it was she who was revealed as a petty thief.

He got out of the shower, got dressed, and took a deep breath. Thomas mustn't see me cry, he thought. But when he entered Alexandra's apartment, Thomas immediately asked, "Why does your face look sad, Uncle Iron?"

Iron knew he couldn't hide the truth from the boy. He smiled and said, "You're right, Tommy, I'm sad, but don't worry. It'll pass."

Thomas had been handsome and perceptive from the time he was an infant. His mother had passed her blue eyes and light hair to him. From Max, he received the shape of his face and his height. Alexandra had been both mother and father to him, but as soon as Iron had entered their lives, the heart of the toddler was captured by Iron's strong arms and broad chest. Every time Iron entered the apartment, Thomas ran to him, held onto Iron's solid legs with his short arms and buried his head in his knees.

And Iron? He was born to be a father. Everything his own father had denied him, he granted to the cub who had adopted him. Iron taught Thomas to look into the eyes of the animals on the street, to catch their gaze. "If she's good, tell her you love her. Not with your mouth, with your eyes."

"And if she's bad?" asked Thomas.

"Look away or at the ground and stay out of her way."

"And what should I do after she knows I love her?"

"Then you can easily become her friend." Iron demonstrated this over and over and the boy studied him, and then tried to imitate him. And for the boy who learned to earn the trust of a dog or squirrel in the street, or even a rat, there was no end to his happiness.

## 3

After dinner, Max and Alexandra sat in the living room chairs and each held the same book. Following the advice of Dr. Greenberg, Alexandra talked to Max about the classics. "If he is interested in the subject, then continue on to the plays," he said.

Alexandra began reading "Crime and Punishment" aloud. And to her immense pleasure, Max, although he showed no signs of being familiar with the work, was interested in it and clearly enjoyed her reading to him. About an hour before midnight, they put down the books and enjoyed a glass of bourbon. Then, they each went to their own bedrooms.

Max lay in his bed. Alexandra ignited within him strong feelings and desire. He picked up the book and continued to read. Alexandra, in her bed, was also unable to sleep. She fought the urge to enter his room and run her fingers through his black hair, to be swallowed up by his body, to be perfumed with his scent which had been imprinted on her heart from the moment he first drew her to him, years before at the Shakespearean theater in Berlin.

The more Max read, the more he knew what to expect from the story. After the murder of the old woman and her sister, the hero would experience unrelenting mental anguish. He knew that only once the hero was sentenced would his troubled soul be quieted. Max fell asleep with the open book in hand. Like virtually every other night, he was awakened from his sleep by the sound of the crazy laugh.

Max was early to the breakfast table. Even the housekeeper wasn't there yet. He walked around restlessly, returned to his room, picked up the book and continued to read. Yes, he had predicted what would happen. The sound of the clattering utensils in the kitchen prodded his hunger. The housekeeper prepared the coffee and he sat down at the table with a wide smile. It worked like a charm, and a fresh roll and cherry jam immediately appeared in front of him.

As he was taking a sip of his coffee, Alexandra entered. He looked at her and his breath caught. Even early in the morning, without make-up, she was simply beautiful. He stood up, bowed to her elegantly and kissed her hand. She smiled, greeted him good morning and immediately asked if he had continued reading.

"Of course," he said, and a flood of words fell from his mouth. "He cannot live with the sin," he said. "He will testify and only once he is sentenced will his soul rest, am I right?"

To her surprise, he knew the book better than she did. Soon his memories will return to him, she thought, and then we can live the life that was meant to be ours.

At that moment, Alexandra Brecholdt did not know how right she was and, also, how mistaken.

# 1926-1929, Berlin

Alexandra had been only sixteen years old when, despite her mother's objections and with the surprising support of her father, she decided to perform as a singer in cabarets and nightclubs. Her father's poor condition placed demands on her mother's time, damaging the functioning of the printing house they owned, making it less profitable. In addition, the money they paid for doctors, medicine, talismans, and spells not only didn't improve the father's condition but diminished their already limited resources.

Although Alexandra's lithe, youthful body and clear voice made her a star in the nightclubs, her heart and dreams ran to the Shakespearean Theater of Berlin. Like many other girls her age, Alexandra fell in love with the star of the play. But, unlike other girls her age, he wasn't a famous athlete, a high-ranking, decorated officer, or a romantic crooner slaying hearts – but Max Fischer, the theater actor.

"He is the greatest Shakespearean actor of our generation!" her father told her when he saw Max Fischer perform the role of Hamlet. The young Alexandra's heart had been snared. She felt an uncontrollable need to know him intimately - to learn him and learn from him, or even simply to be close to him, to smell his smell, to feel the touch of his skin against hers. She was aware of her own beauty; she sensed the looks she received. There were young men who hugged her and even kissed her lips. Her heart raced when it happened. But even when she danced on stage in the "Roma" nightclub with Antony, the handsome Italian dancer, and even when he held her close and stared at her with his big dark eyes – she saw Max's image – only him.

One day, when passing next to the theater, she spotted a notice: "Wanted: singers and dancers for a special production of "Othello" starring Max Fischer and Katerina Roskovska." Her heart soared. She auditioned, and after a week she learned she had been accepted. Although her weekly pay would only be worth what she earned in one successful evening at the cabaret, it was clear to her to which side the scales were weighted.

She did, indeed, dance in the play, and even sang several lines during the scene when Othello is welcomed to Cyprus as a victor, but she did not get to exchange a single word with Max. He was in the habit of going on stage directly from his personal dressing room and returning to it as soon as he left the stage, without speaking to anyone around him.

Every day, she stood backstage, dizzy from his deep voice that transformed on stage from that of a wise, sensitive, good-hearted, and well-loved man – to that of a crazed man. She knew his madness from home. Demons also entered her father, filling him with fears. Day after day, and mostly through the night, he lived with this damned demon. But Max knew how to summon the evil spirit from within him, as well as to part from it with the falling of the curtain, while her father always lived in its shadow.

From the first evening she danced on the theater stage, from the first time she watched him, from backstage, reenacting her father in a fit of madness, Alexandra was driven to run to him, to hug and calm him, exactly as her mother had during the difficult nights.

After every performance, she felt the need to release her emotions with crying; and still, night after night, she imagined herself on stage instead of Katerina, the lead actress, who in her humble opinion – despite the wonderful reviews she received – didn't understand the strength and soul of Desdemona, the heroine of the play, at all.

If only she had been brave enough, she would have invited Katerina to meet her mother, to learn her secrets, the behaviors of a woman married to a man whose soul is shaken, who summons strength in the face of his outbursts of fury. To understand Desdemona, who looked straight at her father, who talked to him quietly and calmly, with a little humor and not a trace of fear. And certainly not the ring of fear apparent in every word uttered by Katerina's Desdemona.

Alexandra did not dare speak, not to Katerina and certainly not to Max. She continued to hope that maybe, one day, she would have the courage to do so. Max will understand, he will understand what Shakespeare really meant. Indeed, the women in his plays are always strong and take initiative.

Of course, as a rule, life doesn't fulfill the rose-tinted fantasies of young girls. But for every rule, there is an exception.

# July 1945, Munich

## 1

Iron headed towards his apartment, but when he remembered Aishé's intoxicating scent that he would greet him in his empty apartment, he changed direction and headed to a nearby bar. There, he knew he would receive a strong drink, and perhaps meet a lonely woman looking for some company, even if for a moment. There were many lonely women in Munich in those days.

Iron sat down at the bar, exchanged a few words with the bartender and asked for a shot of schnapps. He emptied the glass and asked for another. The bartender put the bottle down next to him. "Drink as much as you like and then pay for what you drank. It looks like you need it, buddy, and what's a shot for a guy your size?"

"Thank you," said Iron. "How much will the bottle cost me?"

"You still work for Frau Brecholdt?"

Iron answered in the affirmative. He was no longer surprised by how well-known he was in the city. The bartender broke into a long monologue about how hard it is to manage a little bar. He complained about the break-ins every week, and the protection money he had to pay. "Between that and the next thing, I haven't got even a single pfennig left," he said.

Iron stared at him for a long moment. He saw fear, despair, and truth. "Why are you telling me all this?" he asked.

"I need partners like you and the lady. Everyone in the city knows not to mess with you. They say you once broke someone's neck with your bare hands."

Iron smiled. He was aware of the reputation he had made, even before he wore the uniform of the Gestapo. "There were two," he said and immediately added in a more serious tone, "Then you also know that the lady doesn't enter into any partnership for less than fifty-one percent."

"I'll accept any offer, even if I'm left with nothing but a salary, as long as I can feed my family."

"No, that's not her way. If she takes the deal, it's always fifty-one percent for her and another ten percent for me. You will continue to work hard so the place will support you. You haven't answered me yet, how much is the bottle?"

"Allow me the honor of being my guest."

"And how much would you take from another customer?"

The owner of the place quoted a reasonable price, and Iron poured himself another glass. Then he looked around and added, "And two more things you ought to take care of before my boss will consider investing in your bar." He pointed at the prostitutes sitting at the bar. "She doesn't and won't step foot in a place where there is prostitution. You can have hostesses who will encourage your customers to drink – but that's the line. Understood?"

The owner nodded. "What's the second thing?"

"There are no more free drinks. Not for me, not for you. Not even for her."

The owner nodded and rushed off to a new customer.

Iron pulled several bills out of his pocket and left them on the counter. He took the half-empty bottle and left. Tomorrow, he would recommend to his boss that she buy the bar, the name of which, and the name of its owner, he hadn't asked.

The desolate street almost reminded Iron of his empty, sad apartment. The exhaustion and alcohol subdued him, but even before he finished turning the key in the lock, he heard noises. Rustling. He did not sense danger, but he opened the door slowly.

The apartment was dark. He pressed himself against the wall, turned on the light and was shocked. For a moment he thought he had made a mistake and was in the wrong apartment. It sparkled from cleanliness, blue silk curtains covered the windows, the furniture had been rearranged and over it all, the air was scented with incense that rose from three smoking sticks. His heart beat rapidly. Aishé. Aishé.

He entered the bedroom. In the bed, between two candles placed on the matching night tables, she slept in a black, silk dressing gown, so thin and beautiful it hurt. "Aishé, Aishé my beauty," he whispered in her ear.

She opened her big eyes, glared at him, and attacked him with her claws drawn. "How dare you come home this late stinking of drink and with a bottle in hand!"

Iron held her hands gently. "I thought you left me, I sat in a bar and tried to forget about you, but it didn't work. And look, you're here, and I am the happiest man in the world."

"You weren't with another woman?" she asked with suspicion.

"No."

Aishé smiled but just for a moment, and her face grew serious again. "Take your clothes off," she said, "Take 'em off. And if I catch the smell of another woman, I'll gouge your eyes out."

"That won't happen, I wasn't with another woman," said Iron and took off his clothes obediently.

Aishé sat on her knees and sniffed his genitals. "You're lucky," she said, "you smell like a man."

Later, Iron woke up with a feeling he had never felt in his life. He found Aishé riding him and looking into his eyes. "Did you dream about me, you big, sweet guy? I wanted you to wake up and find it's not a dream."

Iron smiled and hugged her. "No dream is even close to the real thing," he said, and for the first time in his life he felt the fire of love ignited in his heart. He loved her with all his might and they both fell asleep, smiling.

Iron woke to the smell of coffee wafting through the apartment. In the kitchen he found Aishé with a pan in hand and naked as the day she was born.

"Put something on, I won't be able to focus on the food if you stand there like that."

"I made you an omelet with four eggs, so you won't run out of power," she said and smiled at him. He gobbled up the eggs, swallowed the coffee, kissed her on the lips. "Why didn't you leave me a note? Why didn't you let me know where you went?" he dared to ask.

"For that, you need to know how to write," the girl answered, avoiding his eyes.

"Don't worry, Aishé, if I learned, you can, too," he said and turned to the bathroom. The warm water relaxed his muscles. And then, as he had gotten used to in his childhood, he turned the faucet and a shower of cold water washed over his body.

# 2

Alexandra and Max sat in the kitchen and talked. They look as if they are close, thought Iron. He refused the breakfast the housekeeper offered him, which earned him a closer look from Alexandra. But he did agree to drink a cup of coffee with them, even though it was thin and weak compared to what Aishé had prepared.

"You were in the middle, don't let me bother you," he said and sat down.

The moment of quiet was interrupted by the ringing voice of Thomas, who burst into the room riding on a broom. "I don't need a bicycle either, Uncle Max," he called loudly.

All eyes in the room turned towards him. The resemblance between the boy and Max, who had ridden the broom the same way two days earlier, was not lost on Alexandra or Iron, but Max ignored what was plain to see and returned to the conversation he was having about the book, "The Count of Monte Cristo." "Dantes will return for vengeance," he said.

"Are you sure you haven't read the rest?" Alexandra asked, hiding her excitement with difficulty.

"I haven't read it," Max answered. "Maybe I'm reminded of things I once knew?"

Alexandra's heartbeat quickened, but she only shrugged. "I don't know," she answered. "Time will tell." She looked back at her son who, aside from his blue eyes, was a small and joyful copy of his gloomy father.

Iron studied Max's eyes. Loneliness and sadness filled them, but something else had been added. Hope? Joy? He couldn't completely decipher it.

"I need to talk to you a minute about work," he said to Alexandra. "Yesterday I located a bar you should invest in."

Max immediately got up from his chair. "I'll let you talk quietly," he said and went to his room.

"What the hell was so important that you had to interrupt our conversation for a new bar?" Alexandra asked angrily.

"You're on the right track..." Iron said and smiled. "Max's animal is getting closer, it wants to speak."

"So, the bar was just an excuse?"

"Yes, of course," Iron answered. "But not just. Five minutes' walk from here, there's a bar I visited. The owner works there himself, an honest man..."

"You know I don't..." Alexandra started to express her opposition.

"I told him. Fifty-one percent for you, ten percent for me, get rid of the prostitutes, and he has to stay and run the place."

Alexandra smiled. "I knew I needed you as my right hand. Now tell me what or, more accurately, who you're hiding in your apartment."

Iron blushed, "Am I that transparent?"

"You?! Iron?! Refuse breakfast? There is only one reason that could happen; you already ate a decent meal. And if that's so, then I would like to know who is responsible." Alexandra laughed heartily.

"Her name is Aishé. She's beautiful and good and she loves me."

"And you?"

Iron searched for the words to answer her and couldn't find them. How could he tell her he had only discovered what love is that night? "I thought I loved you..." he stammered. "But this feels different... maybe because I never had a family... maybe I love you like one loves a big sister... with Aishé, I feel like she's part of me. I have a fire burning in my heart. Yesterday, for a few hours, I thought she had left me, and it hurt so much… is that love?"

"The greatest writers and poets have tried to describe love and didn't succeed. But I understand you, because I knew true love with Max." Alexandra hugged him hard. "Thank you for your honesty, you are truly the little brother I never had. I really hope you found a good woman, and I want her to come to dinner. I will not accept a refusal." Iron stood and flexed his muscles, "Who are you calling little?" They both laughed.

Iron left the room relieved.

# August 1945, Munich

## 1

Alexandra decided to gradually switch from reading books to reading plays they had acted in together. Every book Max read ignited a new memory. She felt the warmth between them, Max frequently touching her hands, his hidden looks. With the months passing, she wanted him more and more. Not only his physical closeness, she desired Max's love, the Max who knew her. And another thing bothered her - when would be the right time to tell Max about his son? About Thomas?

And so, one evening, after they had drunk one glass too many, Alexandra's patience burst.

"You don't see the resemblance between you and Thomas? He really looks just like you," she erupted.

Max recoiled. His pupils dilated and his eyes began to race from side to side as if he were searching for a hidden enemy. His breathing sped up, and his face was washed in a cold sweat. "No! No!" he screamed. "Not my son!" he got out of his chair as if he were facing an enemy.

Alexandra held his shoulders gently. "Relax, it's me, Alex, me and you."

Max stared at her blankly. His eyes rolled back in his head and he collapsed to the floor like a ragdoll. Alexandra reached for his neck and checked his pulse. "Max!" she cried, "Max, wake up!" She slapped his cheek and shook him gently.

Max opened his eyes and looked at her confused. "What's happening to me?" he asked frustrated, "When will this laugh stop making me crazy? When?"

## 2

Alexandra led him to his room, and then hurried downstairs to Iron's apartment. She knocked on the door. She had to talk to him as quickly as possible.

She heard a woman's voice on the other side of the door, but before she was able to absorb what she had said or in what language, she found herself standing in front of a young, exotic woman. Aishé was dressed in a completely transparent black silk nightgown, and she peeked out curiously from elongated, purple eyes that stood out against her skin. Alexandra smiled and remembered the fresh scratches that appeared on Iron's face several days earlier; she realized she was standing in front of the woman who was responsible for them.

"You must be the boss lady," Aishé broke the embarrassment.

"Ah y – es," said Alexandra, "I'm looking for..."

"Oh no! Same story? You and me looking for Iron?" Aishé laughed.

"I see he's not here..."

"You think I would open the door dressed like a whore in your honor? I thought it was him."

"It's... okay... you surprised me, but I'm sure I surprised you even more. Do you know where he is?"

"He said he was going to visit a new bar in the area."

"Please tell him I was looking for him. In essence… it can wait till morning."

"Frau Brecht…" Aishé got tangled in the name and stopped short. "Uh, Alexandra… if it could wait, you wouldn't be here now. Sit. I'm making us coffee."

"Thanks, but I really don't want to impose, and it really can wait till morning… and it's, it's okay, you can call me, Alexandra."

"You wanted to talk. I'm here, listening," Aishé said. She filled a small kettle with water, added two heaping teaspoons of coffee grounds and a teaspoon of sugar and put it on the stove. When the water started to simmer, she added a trickle of cold war to stop the boiling. She did this five times. Alexandra watched the unfamiliar ritual with curiosity. The aroma of the coffee wafted through the room. Aishé waited several minutes before she poured it into small porcelain cups.

"The cups are lovely," Alexandra said and tasted the thick coffee." The scalding, concentrated liquid passed her throat and her eyes widened. "You must teach me how to make it like this!" she said.

"Forget about that for now, tell me," Aishé whispered. And Alexandra did. She told her about the days of her childhood, about her parents and about Max Fischer. She told the story of her love for him, her love of the theater, about the pregnancy, the birth and about Thomas.

"So, Thomas, who Iron loves so much, is Max's son?"

"Yes…"

"You know Max is totally crazy about you?" Aishé asked.

"I don't know what's going on in his head today…" Alexandra mumbled.

Aishé was silent and looked at her with concentration. "No…

well..." For a moment she hesitated, and then the words exploded from her mouth. "You haven't fucked since he got here?"

Alexandra blushed, and suddenly felt very close to this woman she had just met. "Honestly, no," she said. "Although I wanted to, I want to, but I'm afraid of how he'll react."

"What are you waiting for? A woman wants – a woman takes. And the body? It remembers even if the mind forgets. When his body knows who you are, maybe it will remind his blank mind." Alexandra stared at her and didn't say a word. "Excuse my language, I'm a simple woman, a Gypsy. That's how we speak. And you, you can sit here, you're welcome to, but it would be a shame to waste the time, Mrs. Alexandra. Iron said that Max is your man, and that you love him. My Iron knows to do almost anything, but he can't do this work for you... go home, go to him, tear off his clothes, and love him like a woman loves a man."

"Now? After everything that's happened?"

"Do you know a better way to calm a hysterical man?" Aishé stood, went to the door, opened it wide, and whispered in a warm voice, "Go, Alexandra, go get your life and your man's life back."

Alexandra took several steps towards her and fell into her arms. Tears streamed from her eyes. "Thank you, my sister, thank you."

"Go, go to him, Alexandra, and may the gods of love go with you."

# 3

Alexandra got undressed, put on a nightgown, and got into her bed, but she was all worked up. The words, lacking any kind of falsehood, rolled around in her head. They ignited a flame within her. But what if I frighten him, like what I said about Thomas frightened him?

"Go," said Aishé, "Go, the body remembers..." The words returned and burned in her head.

She stood up in front of the mirror, dropped her gown to the floor, and looked at her naked body. The birth and her age had deepened her beauty. She ran her hands over her breasts. Her body burned. She put the red nightgown on again and walked decisively to Max's room hoping the door to his private quarters was not locked.

In the dim light she saw Max sleeping peacefully on his back. She went to him, pulled down his trousers and gently stroked him. She pressed her lips to his and inhaled the scent she had never forgotten. His hands reached for her body, touched and caressed her. "My Desdemona... Desdemona my love, where have you been?" he whispered as if in a dream and his body trembled. She kissed his cheeks lightly, and he smiled. "My beloved woman," he whispered and fell asleep.

# 4

The dawn light streamed through the slats of the shutters and Max realized he had overslept. The previous day's events passed before his eyes as if they were happening that very moment: the nightmare that had disturbed him, so vivid and alive and more horrifying than any he had before - a man with no face aimed a pistol at a scarecrow shaped like a child, a scream from nowhere and everywhere, the ringing crack of a shot, and then the laugh, the same ceaseless, horrible laugh that woke him and haunted him, even once he was awake.

And she had also been there, like always in his dreams - a woman or an angel who floated above him and silently disappeared just after the shooting. But this time she didn't disappear. She woke him just before the shot rang out, and he called her Desdemona. And when he woke – she was there, kissing, hugging, nibbling, petting, licking, loving, chasing away the terrible laugh from his ears, banishing the remnants of the nightmare. And he recognized her, the angel-woman, and loved her. And he didn't even know her name. "My Desdemona," he called her when his organ took control of his tongue. Yes, that's exactly what he yelled, "Desdemona, my love," and his senses clouded.

When he came to a little later, he found next to him his benefactor, Alexandra Brecholdt, the woman he desired and even loved in the light of day. How and when had the routine of his smiling days merged with the darkness of his nightmare-saturated nights? How had the angel's figure from the dream been replaced by the figure of Alexandra from life? He only hoped he hadn't offended her when he called her by the name of another in the moment when the darkness succumbed to light, and the nightmare became a waking dream. Maybe she had been offended, Max worried. Indeed, when he awoke with the dawn, she wasn't there. She got up and left when he fell back to sleep. Perhaps it had all been a dream? But no, it was not a dream, Alexandra Brecholdt had come to him in his sleep – indeed her sweet smell still infused the sheets of his bed, mixed with the scents of love. She woke him, loved him, and he loved her. So why had she gotten up and gone? He had to find out, to try and understand who and what was Desdemona.

Since the time when the insane laugh first woke him in those cursed barracks, he had never felt so alive, and yet so confused and afraid. Love, hate, fear, and hope all fought each other in the depths of his tormented mind.

## 5

His whole life, Iron had never encountered a case like this. Max's soul, the primal animal according to his philosophy, was at war with itself.

"Do you want a cup of coffee?" Iron asked. "Alexandra and Thomas went out and the housekeeper has the day off today."

"I have to concentrate," said Max looking confused. "Who is Desdemona?" he asked, distracted. "Do you know what book she appears in?" Iron shrugged and Max strode over to the library and began searching through the books on the shelves until he gave up and sat down in one of the armchairs. "Leave me alone, please," he said to Iron. "I need a little quiet."

Iron heeded his wish, left the apartment, and went downstairs to wait for Alexandra on the street, as they had planned. Only several minutes passed before he saw her walking towards him.

"Thomas is at school, tell me, tell me what he said," she pleaded.

"He's very close," Iron answered.

"Stay in the area, I may need you," she said and hurried home.

As soon as she entered, Max wrapped her in his arms. She responded warmly to his touch, which led in a moment to a kiss. When their lips parted, he whispered in her ear, "Please don't be angry at me for calling you by another woman's name. I don't even know who Desdemona is, or why I called you by her name."

"Don't worry, I have always been and always will be your Desdemona," she answered. She said the words with confidence, but her soul was in turmoil.

"I want to know her."

"Then you will," she said and pulled the play, Othello, from the library shelf.

"Start reading. I'm going to rest and we will meet this evening."

# 6

That night, after the house was quiet, the two sat opposite one another. It had been a long time since she had last played Desdemona, fighting for her life with Othello who was immune to the logical and loving words she spoke to him. The words reminded her of her mother, and that memory infused her with strength.

"You be Othello, read from the point where you stopped, I will be Desdemona."

He began to read. He read like someone encountering the text for the first time. She answered with the diction and emotion she knew.

"Continue, continue the dialogue until the end of the scene."

And he continued. She delivered her lines and he read his. When they reached the end, Max exclaimed, "He went crazy? She loves him, why did he strangle her?"

"Again, read from the beginning of the act," Alexandra directed.

And he read again, and again she answered and again she was Desdemona with the same power, with the same courage, as when she was in the theater in Berlin.

It happened in a moment, right before her eyes. Max became Othello, the same wild and miserable hero who struck in a mad fit of jealousy, sentencing his wife, and himself, to death. He put down the book and performed before her, exactly as he had that night in the dressing room, and just as he had hundreds of times on stage.

# February 1930, Berlin

## 1

It happened one evening. Barely an hour before the curtain was to go up, Katerina, the lead actress, tried to avoid the mud sprayed by a car passing in front of the theater and she slipped on the ice. She sprained her ankle. Her understudy, who sat each night in a booth backstage and prayed for exactly this, had, as she had every night she wasn't called upon to perform, systematically emptied a bottle of schnapps. And because she started drinking a full hour before the curtain rose, in her state, she could perhaps play a drunken sailor in a pub, but there was no way she could deliver the sensitive dialogue of Shakespeare.

There was a commotion in the theater. The general sense was that the evening's performance would be cancelled. It was the moment Alexandra had been dreaming of the moment when she must take action.

She knocked on Max's door, entered and asked him to listen to her for a moment.

Max looked at the beautiful girl and answered with a smile, "It looks like I have nothing better to do at the moment - speak to me, child."

Alexandra looked straight into his eyes and in a quiet, sure voice, spoke Desdemona's response to Othello's threat to kill her, words she had practiced dozens of times in front of her parents and before her bedroom mirror,

> "That death's unnatural that kills for loving.
> Alas why gnaw you so your nether lip?
> Some bloody passion shakes your very frame.
> These are portents; yet I hope, I hope,
> They do not point on me."

She sounded just as she wished, like a strong woman who doesn't understand what's taken hold of her beloved and tries to calm his stormy soul and even joke with him. The amused look disappeared from Max's eyes and became the mad glare of Othello, "Peace, and be still!" he answered. In the short sentence there was a kind of hesitation. Not the same anger he expressed on stage opposite Katerina. The girl's blatant self-confidence that appeared out of nowhere, shook his confidence. The girl in his dressing room had transformed into Desdemona, she, who despite her strength, Shakespeare sentenced to be murdered night after night, on stages across the globe.

"I will so. What's the matter?" she asked in wonder.

Max skipped ahead several lines. "Thou art on thy deathbed... confess thee freely of thy sin... Thou art to die."

Alexandra immediately answered, "Then Lord have mercy on me!"

Max raised his hand to silence her. "You understand what you're doing, child?"

"Yes, is it no good?"

"Does it make sense that a young woman wouldn't fear the rage of a warrior threatening her?"

Alexandra fought with all her might to prevent the desperation from creeping into her voice. "She loves him, she knows he loves her, why should she be afraid? She has to calm him, not beg him."

"You... know the entire role by heart?"

"Yes, the whole play, all the female roles in all of Shakespeare's plays."

While he was still entranced by her beauty and the vitality she embodied, the door opened.

"I'm sorry Max, it seems, that..." The theater manager stopped mid-sentence. His eyes fell on Alexandra. "You? The dancer? Who gave you permission to be here in Max Fischer's room? Do you even know who Max Fischer is?"

Startled, Alexandra retreated to the door.

"Just a minute," said Max, "Don't go." A decision took shape. "I request that the company prepare to take the stage," he added.

"But we have no Desdemona!"

"I have a Desdemona. What's your name, girl?"

"Alexandra. Alexandra Brecholdt," she mumbled, not believing the sound of her ears.

"You hear? Alexandra Brecholdt will play the role of Desdemona," Max said smiling at his manager. "Now both of you get out of here, I have to focus."

"I hope you know what you're doing..." the manager muttered and hurried out. Alexandra left after him.

"Call make-up and wardrobe immediately so they can prepare the girl for the role of Desdemona," he called and went out on stage before the audience.

"Honorable ladies and gentlemen, we are sorry to inform you that Katerina Roskovska has had an accident and will not be performing this evening. But to our good fortune, a daughter of our city, Max

Fischer's favorite student, is with us visiting him from New York where she is the star of the Shakespearean theater. Without any advance notice, she agreed to fill the role of Desdemona this evening. I am pleased to inform you that tonight, appearing on stage in the role of Desdemona is Alexandra Brecholdt!"

He smiled at the scant applause that rose from the audience and disappeared backstage.

"A smart man, that manager of ours," Max said to the make-up artist. "He knows how to turn vinegar into wine. I just hope that it's not, in fact, vinegar."

## 2

Alexandra took the stage and played a young, daring Desdemona. As the play unfolded, more than a few tears were spilled by the moved spectators. In the climactic moment when Othello leans towards Desdemona to grab her neck, she threw her head back as if to invite him to choke her. Max, surprised, hesitated a moment, and then regained his composure and clenched her neck. He sensed the audience holding its breath. His breath also stopped a moment. He knew he was performing with the finest Desdemona he had ever encountered.

## 3

The reviews, as reviews tend to be, were divided. There were those who could not heap enough praise, while others skewered Alexandra. Some claimed this performance was a significant step forward in the theater world and some countered, with the same fervor, that a young, impertinent girl played a light-hearted Desdemona inappropriate for respectable theater. One way or the other, word about the new Desdemona spread through Berlin like wildfire. The audience swelled, and every performance was sold out ahead of time.

However, Alexandra was not interested in her growing salary, nor in the success she garnered. The only reviews that mattered to her were those of her father and Max Fischer. They both praised her interpretation of the character and the performance that captured hearts. Her father, who already saw the show with her mother the second night she appeared in it, was at his happiest. "I have won, we have won, Claudia," he said to his wife. And Max said, "The best Desdemona I have ever played opposite, the most unique." And added, "I yearn for the moment you will play opposite me in 'Taming of the Shrew' or 'Hamlet.'"

What more could she have wanted? Her dream had been fulfilled almost in its entirety. Only two things tempered her happiness – her father's psychological condition, and Max's impending marriage to Berta.

# 4

'Othello', starring Max Fischer and Alexandra Brecholdt, ruled the Berlin Theater stage for over a year. Katerina, who healed from her sprained ankle, became Alexandra's understudy and, on the evenings when she performed, the theater was half-empty. In the following plays produced by the theater, Alexandra played the female lead opposite Max. Before his eyes, she transformed from a girl into a woman - an amazing woman, smart, hypnotic in her talent for dancing and singing, and an actress unlike any he had ever met. She could be soft, whispering and spoiled, but she could also be a hissing street cat, scratching and biting. Her gaze radiated hate or disdain and the audience sensed it.

Max tried to blind himself and inure himself to her gaze, but his heart was captivated by her - not a small problem for a man who was engaged to his childhood sweetheart, Bertha Gottlieb. Max and Bertha had known each other since they were small, and their close friendship blossomed into true love in their adolescence, a love their parents welcomed. Bertha's father, Manfred Gottlieb, was an art dealer and a generous theater patron, which was helpful to Max in the early days of his career. However, it wasn't this fact, rather his genuine love for Bertha and the knowledge that breaking off the engagement would crush her, that hardened his heart to the love of the new star who had suddenly appeared in his life.

And so, just after 'Taming of the Shrew' closed and before the opening of 'Midsummer Night's Dream', despite the economic crisis that had Germany in its grip at the time, the wedding of Mordechai Max Fischer to his beloved Bracha Bertha née Gottlieb was held before a large congregation. And, while the family and guests celebrated, Alexandra Brecholdt lay on her bed, sobbing into her pillow, bitterly.

# September 1946, Munich

Alexandra had created an aperture for light in the dark chasm of Max's mind. She succeeded in awakening his love for her, and even brought back memories of his time in the theater and the plays they performed together. But her hope that this crack in the wall he built around himself would restore his full memory was proven false.

"He is entrenched, like before," Iron told her. "The animal sniffed the light and retreated."

And so, one evening Alexandra asked him, in an indulgent voice, "Max my dear, would you want to perform together again in the theater?"

Max immediately put down the book he was reading and looked at her with concentration. "But I'm not an actor," he said.

"Maxy, we both know you're a highly acclaimed theater actor."

"Maybe I was once, but no longer."

"Then what are you, my love?"

"I'm a clown, that's what I am, I make people laugh."

Alexandra tensed. "Since when are you a clown?"

"Since he told me."

"Who told you this nonsense? What do you mean, a clown?"

In the silence that fell, Alexandra blessed the darkness in the room that prevented him from seeing her body trembling.

"I'm tired," Max said in a sleepy voice, "Tomorrow I'll join Iron. Goodnight."

He went into his room and fell asleep in seconds. Alexandra went in after him, lit the night light next to his bed, and looked at his face for a long time. His sleep was quieter than usual, but her sleep would soon wander to a dark world and a memory she wished to forget.

# January 1934, Berlin

## 1

"I will not take the stage for the premier of Othello, which is returning to our theater after three years, with this... amateur!" declared
Max. "Iago is a smart man, slippery and sly but, most importantly,
sophisticated. How can a primitive bully deceive Othello? And his
thunderous laugh may be fitting in the beer gardens of Munich, but
it is not for the Berlin theater!"

The theater manager has never seen Max so angry and worked
up, but he understood him. Kurt Decker, a member of the Nazi
party and its unit of storm troopers, the SS, was severely limited as
an actor. Max also recognized that he was coarsely courting Alexandra, his prodigy, and that she was not responding.

"You know I didn't really want him, but he came with a recom-
mendation letter from a senior member of the party and no one
on the management board wanted to get into trouble with them.
And you don't want to find the theater burned down one morning.
We're going to have to live with him, this Kurt Decker, and you and
Alexandra will be able to compensate for him."

"It's because of people like you and the board of directors who
give in to them out of fear, that they amass their power," Max said.
"What do we and our culture have to do with these boorish thugs?"

This conversation with the Jewish star didn't exactly please the manager and he shrugged.

"Just make sure we don't hear his psychotic laugh on stage!" Max said.

"And you make sure to educate him like you educate all the others," the director retorted.

## 2

The curtain fell at the end of the opening night, and the applause grew quiet. The actors hugged each other in excitement, champagne corks were pried loose, and cries of rejoicing rose from every direction. Kurt, in the role of Iago, had successfully passed his first test by fire. More than a few members of the audience were sure he was playing a sophisticated parody of evil. Even his thunderous laugh, which he let loose only once, was received with praise. Among the reviews that appeared the next day in the newspapers that toed the Nazi party line, there were those which compared what Kurt brought to Iago with the innovation Alexandra had once brought to Desdemona. Kurt Decker, who essentially played himself, had succeeded in winning over the audience.

Pleased with his success, Kurt planned to celebrate at a restaurant with the rest of the actors. "Alexandra!" he called as she left the dressing room, "Please join us to celebrate the new star in the skies over Berlin!"

"In a minute," she answered, "let's wait for our Othello. Max is still taking the paint off his face."

"He may be able to wash off the black paint, but let's see him stick the little tail he's missing back on!" Kurt responded coarsely and erupted in rolling laughter.

Some of the actors hesitantly joined in his laughter. Others remained angrily silent but did not respond. Alexandra drew close to him with quick steps and slapped him hard across the face. Kurt recoiled, but when he returned to his senses, he got close to Alexandra, grabbed hold of her shoulders, and pulled her to him, his mouth seeking hers. The members of the theater company froze in their places.

"What a hero, let's see you fight me!" Max's thunderous voice was heard.

Kurt let go of Alexandra, turned his head towards Max and spit disdainfully, "Come on, you little Jew!"

Max approached Kurt quickly and threw a punch at his chin, knocking him to the floor.

"Bye everyone, see you tomorrow!" said Max and turned to leave the theater.

Alexandra rushed after him.

"Go, go to your little Jew, you bitch! You'll come crawling back to me, you hear? And he, that clown, will learn his place with his friends with the cropped tails, we'll teach them a lesson yet!" and again Kurt's frightening laugh echoed through the theater.

## 3

"Go away, Alex, it's not the time to stand on the side of a Jew, don't destroy your future because of me." Max's voice was broken.

"No, it's not you and me against Kurt. It's good against bad, light against dark, culture versus ignorance," Alexandra fired off and then fell against his chest weeping.

Max stroked her hair, and just as his mother had calmed him as a child, he whispered in her ear, "Shhh, shhhh…"

Alexandra stopped crying, stared at him with her blue eyes, and whispered, "I love you so much, love you, love you, I don't want anything else in the world." Her lips looked for his, but Max turned his head away from her.

"I'm married," he whispered. "You know that, and Bertha, my wife, is expecting. And even if it weren't for her, and for the baby on the way, it's best you stay away from me, for your own good, Alex my love."

And then he turned his back to her and left the darkened theater.

## 4

The next day, before the performance, the theater manager gathered all the actors and announced in a despondent voice, that Max Fischer had quit. "One less Jew," Kurt snorted disdainfully and laughed loudly. Tears welled in Alexandra's eyes and choked her throat. She slipped silently out the side door of the theater.

Her white breath formed a cloud before her every time she exhaled into the winter cold. It calmed her and dried her tears on her way home. All she wanted was for her mother to hug her and assure her that it would all pass, but Claudia was busy with a different crisis – she was calming her husband, who was screaming in the bedroom. She left the room for a moment, pulled a small bottle from the medicine cabinet, poured some medicine into a cup, and hurried back to his bed, without a glance at her daughter. The sleeping medicine did its work, and he fell asleep.

"You're home early, Alexandra," Claudia said as she left his room.

"Yes, the play was cancelled."

"What happened?"

"Max Fischer quit the theater." Alexandra burst into tears. "He left, I won't see him again, I won't act opposite him." She fell into her mother's arms.

Claudia held her shoulders and pushed her away enough so she could look into her daughter's eyes. "He left because he respects you and loves you," she said. "He is married, my child. He had to leave. One day you'll understand. I know how hard it is for you now, but you will get over it. It's an inescapable part of being a woman, and you're beautiful and smart and an excellent actress. There will be lots more men who fall in love with you, and others that you will love."

"I will never love another man, Mama. I would rather die without him."

Her mother laughed and again held her far enough so she could look in her eyes. "All of Berlin has been talking for years about how you created a different Othello, that the great Fischer became a different Othello once he met you... One doesn't die so fast, my daughter, but overcomes. Time heals all wounds. Now I'm going to sleep, the sleeping pill I gave your father is only good for two or three hours, he'll still need me tonight."

# 1946, Munich

## 1

Max turned to the dining room and found Iron alone. "Where is everyone?" he asked.

"They went shopping," Iron answered.

"We're going out together today, right?"

"Yes," Iron answered and sipped at the coffee in front of him without much desire. "Alexandra told me that you said you're a clown and not an actor."

Max looked at him, and several seconds later, answered, "Yes. To make someone laugh is a special art of its own."

Max took two quick steps forward, slipped, and fell backwards. Iron immediately stood and leaned over him. Max opened one eye and smiled. "Did you throw a banana peel on the floor on purpose?" he asked. Iron burst out laughing. "You know, humor is completely relative. He who looks at the fallen – laughs, while the fallen himself, cries." Max jumped up and left the room with a Charlie Chaplin gait, walking and skipping.

Iron watched Max's back and tried to digest what he had just seen.

"Did you fall, Uncle Max?" Thomas asked when he appeared out of nowhere.

"No, little guy, I didn't fall, I just pretended, to make Iron laugh.

Watch out!" called Max, but too late, Thomas stepped on several marbles, slipped, and fell backwards. Max hurried to him, and the boy looked at him and laughed out loud. "You were mistaken, Uncle Max, you told Iron that the one who looks at the fallen laughs, and you didn't laugh. And I, on the other hand, fell but didn't cry, I'm laughing."

Max looked at him in amazement. "Do you know what you want to be when you grow up?" he asked.

"Yup, either strong like Iron or a clown like you."

Max watched Thomas' back as he strode into the kitchen with Charlie Chaplin's gait, walking and skipping.

## 2

"Tell me what happened," Alexandra asked. She looked completely confused. "He spoke about being a clown again?"

Iron looked at her quietly. "This is, perhaps, the most important and most dangerous advice I'm ever going to give you. Grant him his request, let him be a clown if he wants. Maybe that way he will get his memory back."

"What are you talking about? What did you see?"

"I saw with my own eyes that when he was clowning around, he and his animal became one, a whole person. And what's even more interesting, it was a different person than the tormented Max we know."

## 3

"If you truly want to be a clown, I will help you," Alexandra said to Max. She thought she saw a spark of life flash in his eyes.

"A circus, establish a circus for me. I will be the clown nobody knows. I... I will be Anonymous the Clown!"

Alexandra smiled at how he introduced his name so theatrically. For the first time since meeting her love again, she started to see her old Max in him. His gaunt body had put on weight, his stooped back had straightened, and he looked more alive than ever. A decision took shape in her heart: she would fulfill his request, she would do whatever it took for him to return to her, but one thing still bothered her. "Circuses travel," she said. "What will my role be when you leave me?" "I heard from Iron that you're a wonderful singer, you will sing," he answered with excitement. Alexandra realized that she would soon be a circus owner and for the third time in her life – she would be a singer. And she knew very well who would help her in her mission.

## 4

Iron's famous patience was on the verge of breaking. He stood in front of a long line of clowns, jugglers, animal trainers, and acrobats who answered his ad about the establishment of a new circus. But not a one demonstrated any basic talent in the field he purported to be an expert at. The young man who auditioned for the part of "a special clown," stared at him with calf-like eyes that stood out against his white painted face. Iron waited for something, for movement, for a disturbance in the strange quiet that overtook the room.

And then the young man began to move. He moved forward and stopped, as though he'd hit a wall. An expression of pain rose on his face. He backed away from the imaginary wall, reached forward with one hand, and then the other. It was as if his hands touched the non-existent wall. They travelled to the right until they encountered another imaginary wall which closed in on the man on one side, and then the other. The man moved more quickly from side to side, looking for a way out of the sealed cube. His hands climbed up to discover a ceiling over him, and the more he moved, the more the walls closed in on him. He moved faster and faster – terror visible in his eyes and in every movement of his body. While the imaginary walls closed in on him, he shrank, and his movements became more and more constricted.

Iron watched him, fascinated. He really felt the glass walls closing in on the man and almost got up to help him. Finally, the man sat like a statue, his knees and elbows close together, his head bowed, and he stared straight into Iron's eyes. For a long moment they looked at one another. Iron held his breath, and then saw the smile that twinkled in the young man's eyes.

He released one of his hands between his legs and made a fist. His eyes focused on one point on the "glass wall," and, as if drawing power from an unknown source, he threw his fist forward. His hand passed through the imaginary glass wall, and his face twisted in pain. He carefully withdrew his fist and licked at the non-existent blood. He stood up and bowed to the surprised Iron.

Iron applauded excitedly. "That is not any kind of clowning I'm familiar with, that was amazing!"

In response, the young man bowed deeply, pulled off his hat and passed the length of the room as if he were collecting coins from invisible spectators. From time to time he bit a coin and threw it to the floor with an angry face, until he reached Iron and held out his hat in silence.

"You are mute," Iron said with understanding.

"No, not at all," answered the young man with a foreign accent.

"Where are you from?"

"From France, I was an actor and now I am a mime."

"You have to meet the boss," Iron declared.

"Merci, merci, thank you, you will not be sorry, monsieur… My name is Claude, Claude de Button," said the young man and shook Iron's hand warmly.

"Iron, Iron Mensch."

After weeks of searching, Iron had found a truly special talent.

"Present the same piece to the owners of the circus," Iron directed Claude. However, the next day, Claude walked towards Alexandra and Max and suddenly it was as if he had been caught by a gust of wind. He fought the wind, took a step forward, and was pushed backward again. He held onto his hat as if it were trying to separate from his head, and advanced slowly only to be pushed back again. Finally, he stopped some distance from them, bowed deeply, and cupped his hands together around his mouth as if trying to amplify his voice over the roar of the wind, "I'm Claude, Claude de Button!"

Alex and Max erupted in applause.

"I'm Max and this is Alexandra, very nice to meet you," said Max, and suddenly realized he was yelling, too.

"My apologies, Herr Iron," said Claude, "You told me they were both actors, so I had to do something they could appreciate, something that would be hard for them to imitate."

Iron could see in his eyes that he was being honest.

"I'll check that," Max said and jumped to his feet, but no matter how he tried, he could not imitate Claude's movement against the wind.

"There are muscles you don't develop as an actor," Claude apologized.

But Max didn't smile. "Thank you," he said, "You are excellent, a good choice, Iron. I... I have to rest," he said and left the room.

"Did I anger the boss?" Claude asked with worry.

"You received a compliment from him that few receive. You can relax," Alexandra answered.

And so, the mime was the first to join their circus.

## 5

This success encouraged Iron to double his efforts and continue the search. Three acrobats he hired – a husband, wife, and adolescent son – told him they abandoned a circus parked not far from the Swiss border. "We're talking a whole circus with a tent, wagons, trained animals, and quite a few laborers," the woman said.

"They're all on the edge of starvation," added the father. "You could buy them cheap."

The next day Iron was already on his way to the border. It wasn't hard to locate the circus.

The owner of the circus, an Italian by the name of Carlo, tried to project business as usual, but the gloomy mood that prevailed in the circus tent and the desperation clear in Carlo's eyes, were like the testimony of a hundred witnesses that the situation was as bad as it could be.

"Tell me what happened," Iron asked gently, and the two sat on a bench. "Maybe we will be able to help each other."

Carlo looked in his eyes for a long time. "I hope you'll believe me," he said. "After having survived the war, with difficulty, I tried to move to Switzerland to perform. I thought I would go from there back to Milano, after years of having not visited. But a group of SS officers who fled from the American army robbed me of everything I had - money, gold, jewelry. They left me here to die with my workers and my animals. Many actors abandoned us. I was left with the animals, their trainer, and a few older performers who can't take care of themselves. You understand, we were like a family… and the animals… one of the elephants has died already, and soon they will all die. Now that you know everything, can you help?" he burst into tears. Iron didn't have to look into his eyes to know he was telling the truth.

"I won't pay you for the circus," Iron said quietly. "But starting tomorrow, you will receive the whole budget you need to survive. Together, we will move it to Munich, we will rehabilitate it and start to perform."

Carlo stopped crying and looked straight at Iron. "And what will you want from me in return?"

"Seventy-five percent of the circus, and you as the salaried manager for at least another five years."

"Why would you pay for the services of someone who went broke?"

"Because I can see that the animals and the people you're responsible for are more important to you than your own self-interest, and I want to leave you a percentage so it's worth your while to work. Do we have a deal?"

"You won't be sorry, boss, the circus is yours." Carlo held out his hand to shake on it. Iron shook his hand, gave him some money, and continued towards the Swiss border. He had in hand full power of attorney from Alexandra. He sent her a telegram: "I am in Zurich. I bought a circus. We will arrive in Munich within the week."

Alexandra showed the telegram to Max. She may have expected some expression of joy, but there was none. "Thank you, Alex," he said.

## 6

Iron was not familiar with the working methods of the Swiss banking system. Withdrawing the amount he asked for, in American dollars, took more than two days. Carlo was worried he wouldn't return, but he took advantage of the advance Iron gave him to make sure the trucks and wagons were ready to go. And so, to Iron's great pleasure, when he did return, he found the circus ready and eager to travel.

## 7

At exactly the same time that Iron and Carlo were laboring to fulfill Max's whims, Alexandra, Max, and Thomas sat at a table in Thomas' playroom and played a memory game. At first, Alexandra and Max tried to let Thomas win, but they quickly realized he didn't forget a single card once it had been turned over on the table. The game ended when a neighbor arrived and invited Thomas to play on the football field next door with her son.

"Your son has a remarkable memory," Max said. "Just like his mother, who never forgets even a single line of the text."

Alexandra could no longer hold back and asked the question that had been bothering her for days. "Max, my dear, how could it be that you never asked about who the boy's father is? It doesn't interest you?"

"Do you really think I don't see the resemblance between me and Thomas? And why do you even ask when, what you really want, is to tell me something?"

Tears streamed down her cheeks. "So, then you know that you are..." Her words were choked by her crying.

Max got close to her, stroked her head gently and kissed her tears. "I knew it from the first moment I saw him, but I cannot be his father. Not yet."

"Why?"

"I'm still not ready... I... it's best that I'm Uncle Max to him or just Max. Not Papa."

In the heat of the conversation, they hadn't noticed that Thomas was still in the room, listening.

"You're my father?" he called happily.

"I'm Max, Thomas, call me Max."

## 8

Carlo stood on the roof of the circus wagon and called out instructions through a megaphone. Iron watched as the central pole of the tent was slowly hoisted upright. As a boy in the circus, he always thought the collection of people who speak an abundance of languages and pull giant poles and bolts of canvas with pulleys and in perfect coordination, were among the giants of earth's wonders. Now, after having amassed some power himself, having seen a thing or two in his life, and becoming a partner in the circus, he still thought so.

Arranged around the tent were the wagons with the animals, the performers and the management car, at the front of which was the ticket counter. Ropes were tightened, stakes hammered in, and additional tents pitched adjacent. Not many hours had passed, and the circus tent stood upright. The stage was finished. Now it was Carlo's turn to cook all the parts together into an enchanting show.

# 1934-1936, Berlin

## 1

To Kurt Decker's despair, it was not he who was chosen to play Othello, but an actor who came from the Vienna Theater. Once he understood that, despite the good reviews he received when he played Iago he would not be granted leading roles, he chose to leave the theater for the sake of a career in the party. This fact made Alexandra very happy, but her thoughts were occupied with Max, who joined – or so she had heard – a movement of artists, most of them Jews, who were fighting the rising power of the Nazi party. They did so through propaganda and education in the poorer areas of Berlin. The economic crisis and run-away inflation created a fertile bed for the seeds of wild incitement planted by ignorant and unbridled nationalists among the weakened population. Anti-Semitism swelled, and the group was often confronted with violence.

At the same time, Alexandra won dizzying success, which brought with it publicity, and the publicity brought money. The theater which had lost its great star now had a female star. Influential citizens of the city invited her to give private performances for significant pay, and a large part of her earnings were dedicated to supporting her father's treatments. To her and her mother's joy, his situation improved, and the anxiety attacks and fits of rage he experienced became less frequent.

Alexandra was twenty-four years old, independent, affluent, beautiful, and available. Is it any wonder that the young men of Berlin sought her companionship? But not a one conquered her heart, which was completely devoted to another man, the love of her youth.

The theater – after Hitler's rise to power – was given new life and new audience members, mostly clad in black uniforms and with red armbands branded with a swastika in their center. Many plays and shows were ruled illegal, Jewish actors were denounced and banished from the theater. Most of the plays performed were appropriate for an ignorant audience but allowed Alexandra to show off her dancing and singing skills. Sometimes, while dancing on stage in front of the strange audience, she was glad Max was not there watching her with his penetrating eyes, knowing her soul, the soul of an actor. As a daughter of the German nation, she worried that she would no longer be able to look him in the eyes, as if she, herself, were guilty of his situation.

## 2

The theater actors were not surprised to receive notice about the planned meeting. In those days, meetings were held daily. With the completion of the evening show, Kurt Decker entered the theater, accompanied by his entourage in shiny, pressed SS uniforms.

"Hello colleagues," he said. "I've missed you. Those of you who are new here, may not know that I was among the best of the actors at this theater and it is, therefore, dear to my heart. You are important not only to me, but to your country and our nation. You are a part of the dissemination and the implanting of the Aryan culture among all our citizens and in the glorification of our name throughout the world."

His gaze wandered over the actors and focused on Alexandra. "I have come to thank you in the name of the country and the party, and now I wish to talk with the lead actress. You are dismissed!" Kurt clicked his heels and raised his arm in salute. "Seig Heil!" he cried and his assistants and a few of Alexandra's colleagues stood and returned, "Heil Hitler!"

Alexandra stayed seated, ignoring Kurt's lustful gaze.

"Good evening, Miss Brecholdt," he said once the hall had emptied.

"To you too, Mr. Decker."

"It's a pleasure to meet you again after all the time that has passed. How do you feel here without me, and without, what was that Jew's name, Fischer? Yes, Max Fischer." He paused a moment. Alexandra remained silent. "You know I owe you my gratitude, right?" Alexandra looked at him, confused. "It's because of you that I reached my standing in the party," he gestured at the stripes on his uniform.

"Because of me? I don't understand."

Kurt laughed his satanic laugh. "You don't think I know that I didn't receive the roles commensurate with my talent because the prima donna of the theater, Alexandra Brecholdt, refused to perform opposite me?"

A wave of chills climbed Alexandra's spine and up the back of her neck. She may have hated the stage while he stood on it, but she never tried to block his path. She felt a wave of nausea and tried to hide it from his attentive eyes. The slap she delivered to his face, echoed in her ears. "I never..." she started to say, but Kurt cut her off rudely. "Don't worry, it all worked out for the best. I invested in the party, and you see where I have gotten." Again, he pointed proudly at his rank and laughed a moment, and then grew serious and shot her a penetrating look. "Do you still see the Jew?"

"Who do you mean?"

"Don't play games with me, you know very well who I mean. I mean the one they had to stop me from killing with my own hands."

Alexandra blinked. For a moment she was again an actress on stage. "I wouldn't dare play with a senior officer of the SS. You mean Fischer?"

"Yes."

"Indeed, you were here when he left, I haven't seen or heard from him since."

"You know he had a son?" Kurt saw the surprise in her eyes.

"No," said Alexandra.

"Excellent, let it stay that way. Your parents own a print shop, correct?"

"Y –es," she stammered, and a warning light went on in her mind. "Why do you ask?"

"Your father still pretends to be sick from the war? Still a parasite?"

Alexandra bent her head. She knew Kurt was trying to shake her confidence and anger her. "My father is not pretending, he is sick, psychologically disabled, he is not a parasite. He gave to the country to the best of his abilities."

"Wonderful. You know that someone like me can help him and the printing house a lot." No, she would not take the bait. She would say nothing.

"If you prove your loyalty to the Reich, the Reich will help you."

"I try, honorable captain. I can only do my part in the theater, that's all I know how to do."

"Your Jew is an enemy of the Reich and of the Führer, he incites the public against the elected government, and we are aware of his activities. If you discover his hiding place, will you report it?"

"Yes, honorable Captain."

"We, I, can help, but we can also cut off your career and destroy your daddy's printing house. Remember that."

"Yes, I will remember, honorable Captain."

"Call me Kurt. After all, we're friends, colleagues, no?" He laughed his mad laugh.

**3**

Alexandra strode home on foot. She needed the crisp air to digest the conversation. Not only was she worried about her family's fate, the fate of her parents and their ability to make a living, but she realized they were looking for Max, to whom a son had been born. Max's son, she thought, and her stomach turned. She must warn him, and maybe she could even arrange for him and his family to be allowed into America. Once, Max had taken her to his uncle, a tailor who worked in Berlin, to shorten the sleeves of her dress. On their way there, he told her his uncle was not just a simple tailor. Because of his familiarity with the Jewish community, he could locate any Jew in Berlin.

Although Alexandra was absorbed in her thoughts while walking, she noticed a man following her. She pulled a cigarette out of her bag and pretended to rifle through it. "Excuse me, sir, perhaps you have a match?" The man hesitated and then drew closer to her and took a matchbook out of his pocket. He lit a match and held it out to her. "Thank you. Were you at the theater?" she asked.

"Yes, Miss Brecholdt, you were wonderful, I waited for you to come out, I wanted to ask for your autograph, but I was too shy." He held his program out to her.

"Don't be embarrassed. What's your name?"

"Friedrich."

Alexandra pulled a pen out of her bag and wrote, "To Freidrich, continue to enjoy good theater, Alexandra." She handed it to him.

"Thank you," he mumbled and turned away.

Alexandra continued to walk circuitously until she was sure Friedrich was not on the horizon, and that no one was following her. She hurried towards the city center and reached the tiny shop of the tailor. The shop was closed, but she remembered that the mending itself he did at home, on the floor above the shop.

"Who's there?" a weak voice answered her knock on the door.

"It's Alexandra Brecholdt, please open the door for me, Mr. Fischer."

Fischer the Tailor opened the door and peered out cautiously. "Sorry for my behavior, it's hard for a Jew here and now."

"I understand," said Alexandra, and immediately added, "I have to get a message to your nephew, Max. Can you help me? It's a matter of life and death." The tailor nodded without uttering a word. Alexandra again took out the pen, asked for a piece of paper and an envelope and wrote a short note. She slid the paper into the envelope and sealed it. "For your own sake, don't open it," she said.

With the flood of emotion, Alexandra had forgotten the ball marking the opening of the theater's 1936 season. She got into a taxi and hurried home. Her parents, dressed in their finest evening clothes, waited for her impatiently. Alexandra apologized and hurried to get ready. The moment she finished her make-up, she heard the car of the young Baron von Basarab come to a stop outside the house. In keeping with his station, he arrived exactly on time. The baron stepped out of the car in a black tuxedo, a white shirt, and a bowtie. He opened the passenger door and waited for her.

Alexandra and her parents left the house and turned to the car.

The young baron opened the two back doors and greeted them. Alexandra sparkled in her shiny black dress, a white scarf wrapped around her neck and a small black hat with black tulle that perfectly set off her wavy blond hair that spilled below her bare shoulders. Black heels completed the look.

The baron smiled at her. "You're more beautiful than ever, my dear." He kissed both her cheeks.

"Please meet my parents, Claudia and Helmut Brecholdt," she said.

"Baron Claus von Basarab the Third," said the baron, bowing deeply.

The gala audience stood on both sides of the red carpet at the entrance to the theater and applauded the theater star and her handsome chaperone. "In your rosiest dreams, Helmut, did you imagine the whole theater world of Berlin would gather for our daughter?" Claudia smiled at her husband.

"I didn't dream of it, and look how perfect they are for one another," he added. But the pall in Claudia's eye suggested she didn't share her husband's opinion.


## 4


Fischer the Tailor may not have known where Max was, but the Jews had their own channels of communication and at their heart was the synagogue. On Saturday morning, Fischer the Tailor arrived at the synagogue with the sealed letter in his pocket. He whispered what he whispered into the ear of someone, and then stood not in his usual place, but in the last row. After about an hour, Yank'l stood next to him and whispered to him, "I understand you're looking for Mordechai." Fischer the Tailor nodded. "I don't know where he is, but I can get the message to him."

Fischer the Tailor nodded again. He knew Yank'l and knew he could trust him. No one saw the sealed letter change hands.

## 5

I'll wait every other day near the side entrance, an hour after the curtain falls. It's important that you come. A.

Max read the note that arrived in a sealed envelope and was slipped surreptitiously into his pocket by someone who quickly disappeared afterwards. He turned it over and over, wondering why it was important that he come. He hadn't gone into hiding without reason. He knew his opposition activities were known to the authorities and that they were looking for him. He was afraid of a trap, but it was written in Alexandra's familiar handwriting. His deep yearning for her and the slim chance they would ambush him at the theater where he used to work were the deciding factors.

He dressed in one of the costumes he used when he went out. This time he wore thick glasses, a little mustache, bushy eyebrows, and make-up to put a little white in his black hair, making him look about sixty. He arrived at the theater an hour before the curtain went up, bought a ticket, and entered the theater.

## 6

It was enlisted theater of the worst kind - a patriotic amalgamation of nationalism, race, and marches. And there was Alex. Older than he remembered her, so beautiful it hurt, and talented as a devil. She played a mother instilling courage in her son who was about to go to war for his homeland, just as mothers were wont to do in ancient Sparta. "Do not fear the bullet, your fate is already written, it's good to die for your country!" she cried with pathos.

Max wondered if any of the spectators, most of whom were in uniform, understood the double message Alexandra conveyed; on the one hand, blind patriotism to the fatherland, and on the other, a sharp anti-war message. The play reached its climax when the mother was informed of her son's heroic death, and she sang his praises to the audience in a bell-like voice that rose to a heart-breaking wail and dropped to a whisper. The moment she finished her song and the curtain fell, the audience erupted – Max among them – in wild applause. And while the audience filed out of the theater, Max turned to the door that led backstage. He calmly passed the actors who skittered past in different stages of nakedness and continued to stride confidently towards Alexandra's dressing room. He knocked on her door. "Who is it?" her melodious voice rang out and immediately touched his heart strings. For a moment he was ashamed for thinking that maybe she had set a trap for him, and therefore had come an hour before the one she specified in the note.

"Me."

The door opened immediately, and Alexandra recoiled. "It's me," he repeated and pulled off the thick glasses. Alexandra blanched, looked around to see if anyone stood behind him and pulled him into her room. She went back and locked the door and then fell into his arms. The tears that spilled from her eyes stopped when they kissed, a kiss that, until that moment, had occurred only in her dreams. After a long minute she pulled away from him and then beat on his chest with her fists and allowed herself to cry freely. "I was worried about you, I missed you so much. Tell me, Max, tell me how you are."

Max told her about the son who had been born to him, about the hard times his family was suffering through, so hard, that he was forced to say goodbye to them and live in hiding. He told her about the literature and theater classes he was teaching and about the one-man show he performed for Jewish children in their private homes. "I also established a movement called "Wake up Germany." We are trying to convince the residents of Germany to rise up against Hitler. But the Gestapo is closing in on us, we will have to stop."

"That's why they're looking for you," Alex whispered and pressed a finger against her lips, as there was a knock on the door.

"Are you coming?" the last actor in the theater asked.

"No, my father came for a visit and surprised me. I'll leave with him," she said.

"Okay, see you tomorrow. I'm going. Do you have a key?"

"Yes, thank you, don't worry."

"Last week, Kurt Decker came to visit," she said after several minutes. "He's now an officer of a storm troopers unit. He asked about you. Hinted that he can buoy my parents' business or destroy it… if…"

"If you entrap me?" Max laughed angrily.

"It's not safe for you here. Let me help you escape Germany?"

"I have a family, Alex."

"I'll make arrangements for your wife, and the baby, too. Please say yes, I'm afraid for your life."

"And what about my mother, my father, my brothers, my mother- and father-in-law? I convinced them all not to run away, how can I run now and leave them behind?"

She pressed his hand between both of hers and looked deep into his eyes. "You're not afraid?" she asked.

"Yes, I'm afraid," he answered. "Very much so, and you?"

"I'm afraid I'll never see you again, that this is our last meeting."

"I want you to remember the first moment you entered my dressing room, confused but determined, and you opened with Desdemona's monologue; the moment in which your eyes trapped mind. If I die soon, I'll be sorry only that I did not agree... ah... I didn't want... to... to... I couldn't..." Alexandra shut his mouth with a kiss.

Their hands reached for one another's clothes, tore them off in haste, their lips pressed together. Max took her in his arms, lay her gently down on the sofa and kissed her ears, her neck, her breasts. She hugged him, caressed him, and then wrapped her legs firmly around his waist. "Come to me," she whispered. "Come to me, I've waited for you long enough, come to me Max." Blue stars flickered in his eyes, his mind lost control of his body, of his mouth, of his tongue. "Desdemona!" he cried, "My Desdemona!"

Alexandra and Max lay silent in one another's arms, their breath slowly returning to normal. "Thank you, my love," he heard her voice from a distance, "Thank you, my miserable love." She rolled onto her side and poured them both glasses of the sweet Portuguese wine that stood on the make-up table. "Why did you call me Desdemona?" she asked.

"Maybe because I fell in love with you while you were Desdemona... Even before you played her on stage, when you showed me in the dressing room who she really is."

"You fell in love with me at first sight," she said indulgently. "But I loved you long before that, from the time I was still a girl. I don't even remember from when." Max looked into her shining eyes and took her in his arms. The second time they made love was quiet, calm, and longer than the first. The burning desire was replaced by fervent love and the awareness that this would likely be their last meeting.

"Take care of yourself," she whispered in his ear, "God knows I won't be able to help you anymore."

"We will be together again, you'll see, there is a God in heaven," he said.

For many years, while he was imprisoned, Max thought of those last words they whispered to one another.


# 7


Franz Schmidt, the Gestapo commander of investigations for northern Berlin, picked up the envelope his secretary placed on his desk. The back of the envelope read, "Top Secret. For the recipient only." Franz opened it with trepidation, read the name signed on it, Heinrich Himmler – the honorable head of the SS himself – and blanched.

"Rumors have reached the Führer that a group of Jews who call themselves "Wake Up Germany" ridicule the party and its leader," he read. "It is your responsibility to immediately uncover all the subversive activity that is spreading in your area and put a stop to it." Franz smiled bitterly. He had reported the group himself, a group that presented no danger, nor even a bother to the government or the party, and turned it into "the number one enemy of the government." He should have known that noting Max Fischer as the leader of the group, even if incidentally, would enflame the matter. And still, in order to aggrandize his success, he had turned the little cell into a thorn in the government's side with his own two hands. Franz well knew what would be his end if he didn't succeed in quickly trapping the members of the group. In the hourglass turned over by Himmler's letter, there were only a few grains of sand left. He had to catch Max Fischer and stop him, and he had to do it immediately.

Years before Hitler rose to power, Franz worked at cracking

crime. He ran an intelligence operation of informants who, for a little money or some other pleasure, would even rat out their own parents or children. His network of informants continued to work efficiently for him after he had been recruited by the Gestapo.

Franz called his secretary, Suzanna, informed her he would be out until the afternoon, and asked her to wait for him to return. He went to the center of Berlin in civilian dress and entered a carpet store owned by a Jew, met the owner, and exchanged a few words with him. Then he left the shop, entered a café in the area, and quickly found the man he was looking for. When he returned to his office, he sat in his chair, asked Suzanna for a cup of coffee, and waited patiently. The anticipated phone call came that night.

## 8

At exactly the same time, in a wide living room on the second floor of a house marked with a Jewish star on its façade, a small group of Jewish children gathered. Some of their parents sat in the living room, and some stood just outside it. In the room was a long, folding screen set up to hide the kitchen door, while allowing free passage behind it.

"You're frightened, you rabbit-like Jews, no one dares to stand before me!" A voice rose from behind the curtain. Thus, in the thundering voice of Goliath, Max opened his children's play in which he played both David and Goliath. The screen allowed him to change his helmet, armor, shield, and sword of Goliath for a wig of red hair, the clothes of a shepherd and David's bag. He encouraged the audience of children to yell and curse at Goliath in order to distract him from the stone that was about to be hurled at him and prevent him from covering his forehead with his iron visor. The children happily cooperated, of course, because who in Germany in those days ever asked them to scream to their heart's content?

"So that's it, you understand now, you don't have to despair or be frightened. We are a small nation, but we are smart and brave. The small and smart can conquer the large. In the end, we will be victorious over all the giants and bad guys!" Max finished his speech and the children applauded exuberantly. Max disappeared on his way to his next meeting point.

## 9

Franz Schmidt put down the phone and asked Suzanna to summon Gustav, the commander of his field cell.

"Heil Hitler," said Gustav and saluted with his arm outstretched.

Franz saluted and signaled him to sit. "Good afternoon," he said. "We are pursuing a Jewish underground in accordance with the instructions of Heinrich Himmler, himself. It's crucial you make no mistakes here and that you don't let any one of them slip away –especially not the leader. Prepare a group to head out immediately. Be ready for when I give you the address."

He pulled a photograph out of his drawer of Max holding a skull in his hand. Written on the back of the photograph was a dedication: "Dear Franz, continue to enjoy the theater. Max Fischer." Franz handed the photo to Gustav. He had received it from Max next to the stage door at the end of another successful performance of Hamlet, and it was dear to him. "He's a gifted actor, don't let him fool you and get away."

## 10

Max reached the site of his third meeting that day, disguised as a drunken beggar with a bag in hand. He approached a building where his friends had already gathered, and then he was stopped by an ominous feeling. From his brief experience in the underground, he had already learned not to ignore his feelings. He looked around and easily recognized the Gestapo officers in their new black raincoats and the brimmed hats on their heads. They also turned their heads and looked at the beggar who didn't belong in the Jewish area. Max overcame his urge to avoid the trap. Dogs run after someone who runs, he thought, and was glad he had bothered with the costume he wore. He did not change the direction of his slow limp, and he did not try to hide. On the contrary. Max started to sing a drunken folksong. And he even got closer to Gustav's men and asked if they had seen any garbage lying around. They shooed him away like a pesky fly, and had they not been lying in wait, surely they would have beat him properly. They did not realize that this man who had just turned to them with a tongue heavy from schnapps was the man they were trying to catch.

Max got his distance from them and felt the relief felt by any man or creature who is being chased and succeeds in escaping his predator. The relief was accompanied by deep despair. Max realized that one of his friends had betrayed the group, and that his other friends would be arrested the moment the ambushers realized that he, the head of the cell, had not come. For a moment he considered taking a swig from the bottle of schnapps buried in his bag, that he had used to spread the smell of alcohol around him should he be stopped. He was completely lost in the city that had once honored and respected him, and from which he was now estranged. It had become foreign and hostile.

## 11

"We arrested them all," said Gustav to Franz proudly. It was one short hour after Max had passed right by him.

"All of them? And where is he?" Franz asked, barely containing his anger, and pointed at the picture that had returned with Gustav.

"He wasn't there," Gustav shrugged.

"Did anyone pass in the street while you were hiding there?

The commander of the ambush stared at him. "No, nothing unusual. Jewish mothers and children in baby carriages."

"Did you check them like I instructed you? Did you check that there were really children in the carriages?" Franz asked.

"Yes."

"Anything or anybody else who looked out of the ordinary, who didn't belong to the surroundings?"

"There was a drunk vagabond with a sack picking through garbage. He stank of alcohol and asked us if there was more garbage in the area" The veteran investigator's pulse raced but he didn't give it away, not with his face nor his voice.

"A vagabond in a Jewish neighborhood. What the hell was he doing there? And you didn't stop him to check his ID, or to look what he had in the bag." It was a declaration, not a question.

"Of course not, he wasn't a Jew."

"Yes, of course, and clearly you check that personally...," said Franz. "Keep your people ready and prepare another group to go out immediately.

After about half an hour, Willy entered his office. Franz was happy to see that, despite the late hour, he was as alert as always. He didn't waste a moment on idle conversation and updated his deputy about the events of the last several hours. When he finished, he asked, "Where would you hide if you were in his place?"

Willy Berger, Franz's veteran deputy since the days when they had been detectives in the Berlin police, scratched the back of his neck. "He has nowhere to go, boss," he said after brief consideration. "He saw the team next to the building, he knows his friends were arrested, and apparently, he realizes we knew about the meeting place…"

"That much I also understood, but I left you out of the investigation so you would come with fresh ideas, so you might see what I don't see."

Willy scratched the back of his neck again, and a smile rose to his face. "You said he had a wife and baby?"

## 12

A moment before he drank from the bottle to transport him from awareness to oblivion, Max was hit with a longing for his wife and infant son. He successfully distanced himself from the SS men, made sure no one else was around, and then he entered a dark stairwell. In less than a moment, he changed his costume from that of a drunken beggar to that of a Russian Orthodox priest. A quick glance into his bag confirmed that he had run out of options for camouflage, and he threw it into a pile of garbage. After all, why would a priest have a beggar's sack on his back?

Max hid during the night in a quiet park in the area and, with the sunrise, he approached his house where his wife and son still lived, and patiently lay in wait. His intimate familiarity with the area where he had grown up and lived his entire life, helped him find the spots where he could see without being seen.

After a long hour of expectation, he saw his wife slowly approaching, pushing a carriage with his son, David. About a minute and a half later, he passed next to her and asked in a heavy Slavic accent about a particular address and handed her a note. "Keep your expression frozen, they are probably following you," it said. "Point in some direction and say loudly that you're walking the same way. Afterwards, casually tear up the note and throw the pieces away in different places."

The woman looked at the note and froze. Then she looked at her husband and could not hide the amazement in her eyes when she met his glance. She executed the instructions in the note. Max answered in broken German that he didn't understand. "I'm going in the same direction, you can walk with me," she said. And so, for about a quarter of an hour, Max got to be with his wife and talk to her. He even got to look at his infant son and imprint his image on his heart.

Time, as we know, is deceptive. When they parted, it felt to Max like their meeting had lasted just a split second when, in fact, it had lasted for exactly 18 minutes and 11 seconds. For weeks, months, and even years afterwards, it filled Max's existence for whole nights in which he lay awake and replayed it, minute by minute, word by word, look by look.

## 13

Franz put on a black raincoat, summoned his driver, and joined the ambush next to the Fischer home. He instructed his people not to get near or even to move until they received a sign from him.

When the figure of the Orthodox priest appeared around the corner, Franz recognized the actor who had met up with his wife.

He followed them from a distance as they walked together, and only after they parted, did he instruct his men to arrest him.

Once he was in handcuffs, Franz approached him, smiled, and said, "Hello to you, Mr. Max Fischer, I'm one of your biggest fans."

"Max Fleischer?" Max tried to get out of the trap, but they both knew he was a fawn kicking his hind legs while the lion closed his jaws on its neck.

"I just wanted to cheer up the frightened children…" he whispered as he was pushed into the car.

"And I, all in all, am just doing my job as best I can," the Gestapo officer whispered to himself sadly. Goodbye, and I will not see you again, wonderful actor that I loved. He still did not know that this arrest was about to change his life.

## 14

Alexandra could no longer keep the secret to herself.

"Mama, I have to tell you something," she said that evening, when they sat together discussing the situation in Germany.

Claudia threw her a quick glance and said, "I see something has darkened your mood, what do you want to tell me?"

"I'm pregnant," Alexandra said.

"What?? How? By whom?"

"It's the third month, Mama… and it's Max's." Alexandra burst into tears.

"Oh, my sweet girl, come here," Claudia opened her arms, and Alexandra fell into them.

"I won't ask how and when you managed to see him because I know he disappeared. Don't fret, we will find an excellent doctor who can take care of it…"

"No, Mother, I want this child. It's Max's child, and maybe the only memory of him I'll have left. I'll go away, I'll move somewhere where no one knows me."

"I don't want you to go away. And how will you manage financially?"

Alexandra burst out laughing. "I was going to ask you the same thing."

"We'll get by. I signed a contract with the party. They'll order work from the printing house of half our maximum capacity, and they pay well, and in cash."

"I'll also get by, I'll perform in cabarets, you didn't teach me to sing for nothing…"

Claudia hugged her daughter again. "I'll think of another idea… Something that will keep you close by."

Alexandra sank into her eyes. "There is no other mother like you," she said.

"And I thought you only loved your father," Claudia answered in the same tone and smiled.

The next day Claudia woke Alexandra and said, "I thought about it all night and I have a solution. If we arrange for you and your son, to have a father, no one will say anything…"

"I see you were busy," said Alexandra with a yawning smile. Clearly the conversation with her mother, and the way she had accepted the news, calmed her.

"You need to find a groom, quickly. Someone who will give you and, more importantly, your son or daughter, his name."

"Who would want to marry me in my condition?"

"Those are exactly the kinds of questions that kept me from sleeping all night. I thought, who would want to, or who would it benefit, to marry you now, especially in your condition. You need someone for whom it would be very important right now to marry a woman and get her pregnant as quickly as possible, so no one would know he was a homosexual."

"Homosexual?" Alexandra looked at her mother, and a smile rose to her face. "Mother, you're a genius! I have a good candidate. Almost no one knows about his tendency, and he has already been seen with me more than once in public, a cultured companion, amazingly intelligent, and very respectable..."

"Then I am going to be the mother-in-law of the Baron Claus von Basarab the Third?" her mother smiled.

"He told me, Mama, but how did you know?" Alexandra asked.

"You'll see soon enough, my child, mothers know everything."

"Oh, come on!"

"I saw him look at you at the theater gala, a young man looking at a beautiful woman like you without any desire in his eyes? Does that seem normal to you?"

## 15

"You look wonderful, you are absolutely glowing. But why was it so important to meet in public, at an hour when the chickens still haven't awakened?" the young baron asked right after kissing her cheeks and pulling a chair over for her.

"Even your curiosity can't beat the gentleman you are," smiled Alexandra.

"People watch, I have to play the role I was born into."

Alexandra looked around, smiled a radiant smile, and waved lightly to the familiar faces around them.

"This is a serious conversation, Clausie, but please continue to smile..."

"I'm good at that," the baron smiled and sent an air kiss to an oversized Italian countess.

"Claus, how will you continue to get along here…?" Alexandra asked.

"Like the Jews and Gypsies," said Claus.

"We both know they're living on borrowed time," she said.

Claus shrugged. "I can't change, if that's your question…"

"Oh, come on, of course not, but wouldn't it be better if you were married and a father?"

Claus could no longer maintain his ever-present smile and flashed a piercing look at Alexandra. "A father," he mumbled, "Who would want me as… Alexandra, are you pregnant?"

"And if I am?" she asked.

"If you are, and I am guessing correctly who the father is, we can both save our lives by what I think you're suggesting."

"Exactly. And, therefore, I want you to propose to me, soon," she said.

Claus smiled again at his friend and confidant. He stood up, kneeled on his right knee, and said in a festive voice, "Alexandra Brecholdt, will you be my wife?"

Alexandra, who hadn't expected such a fast reaction, held out her hand in genuine surprise. She stood up, and to the sound of the applause of those sitting at the café, said yes. Someone even pulled out a camera and captured the glowing couple for posterity. That same evening, the picture was published in an issue of "Abend Zeitung."

And this is how the paternal baron learned about his son's engagement, "I want you to come to Munich immediately, you and the actress," he wrote to him.

"I'm afraid my father is against my marriage to you. I know it sounds archaic, but we still only marry other noble families. Father is going to pass the title and the family estate to my younger brother… but if he discovers what I really love, he will disinherit me completely, and that is many times more important than the estate. No one will suspect I'm homosexual if I marry you and we have a baby. It's a brilliant idea…"

"You can thank your future mother-in-law."

As expected, during the visit to Munich, the father clarified to his son that because he was, as he put it enunciating with disdain, "befriending an actress," neither he nor his children would inherit the baronage. Claus, who had been prepared for that, didn't even argue.

Alexandra didn't think for a moment that he would accept her with open arms and take her to his heart. She was prepared for the baron's conversation with her.

"You must think I'm stupid or blind," he said. Alexandra remained silent. "You really believe I'm not aware of my son's proclivities? If they become known to the public – he will be jailed, and I am his father…" Alexandra continued to remain silent. "Therefore, I will continue to support him, both of you, as long as you stay married. But after you separate, I will not support you or the children born to you, is that clear?"

Alexandra leveled her gaze at him, "I do not need anything from you. Everything I need I have received from your son. I do thank you for your honesty."

The wedding ceremony was held near Munich, where the young couple would reside.

"Far from the public eye of Berlin," said Alexandra.

## 16

Max and Alexandra's son, Thomas, was born in January of 1936. Claus played the happy father for about a year, until he met a tall, thin English gentleman and fell in love with him. He packed his things, parted from Alexandra congenially, and moved to London, farther from his father and the homophobic Germany.

Alexandra asked Claus for an immediate divorce, and with it gave up all financial support. She became a divorced, single mother. Thomas was a year old, and they were left alone in an apartment in Munich, for which the elder baron advised her he would not continue to pay. And, in addition, she had a letter in hand from her mother in Berlin which informed her that the printing house's contract with the party had been frozen and her father's treatments were costing them a fortune. Claudia was too proud to ask for her daughter's help directly, but Alexandra did not need a direct request to understand what she had to do.

And so, about a month later in a Munich night club, the announcer got up on stage and announced, "Ladies and gentlemen, the Red Lantern Cabaret is proud to present the premier performance, straight from Berlin, of the most amazing singer in Germany. Please welcome, with a warm round of applause, the Baroness!"

Backstage, Alexandra stood in a sparkling red gown with a plunging neckline and a long slit up her right thigh. In the dressing room, in a carriage, little Thomas slept soundly while one of her friends watched him. Although the stage was Alexandra's second home, she was as nervous as if it were her first performance as a singer. "They'll love me, they'll love me!" she whispered over and over to herself. The orchestra started with a lighthearted melody, and Alexandra – or according to her current moniker – "the Baroness" – burst onto the stage.

# Munich, 1945

## 1

"Manage the show as you see fit," said Iron. "I've spent a number of years in the circus, and I know a good manager when I see one."

"Thank you for your trust. Do you have any special instructions? Things you want or don't want me to include in the show?"

"The owner will also participate in the circus. Mr. Fischer will appear as a clown named Anonymous. No one in the circus may use his real name or photograph him if he is not in clown make-up."

Carlo survived the war because he learned never to ask why. And if he thought, as he did think, that the new owner was hiding his past during the war, he kept that thought to himself.

"And the lady will sing two or three songs every show."

"That's not done in a circus... but she's the boss," said Carlo.

"The animal trainers for the big cats and the elephants are going home today. The animals are afraid of them, they hurt them. The monkey trainer can stay."

"It won't be easy to find trainers who are better than they are..."

"I will fill in for them for now, until you find trainers who will do their work with love."

"You? How would you...?"

Iron smiled gently. "Don't worry, come with me to the tiger cage."

The pair of tigers Carlo had acquired in India, while they were still cubs, were his greatest pride. They survived the period of starvation with the circus and had recovered their strength. Still, their short tempers were apparent in their movements and their angry voices. Therefore, when Iron declared he was going to enter their cage, Carlo hurried to call the trainer and a guard who carried a hunting rifle loaded with tranquilizer darts. Iron instructed Carlo to get rid of the trainer - it was his presence that made the large animals angry - and for the guard to stay outside the cage. Iron instructed him not to shoot without direct instructions from him, and then he approached the cage. He locked eyes with the male tiger and saw the fear in them. Fear of hunger and fear of the return of the painful and humiliating torture he had endured.

I'll be good to you, I'll take care of you, Iron's eyes transmitted to the tiger, and the tiger stared at him with a penetrating and innocent gaze. Look at me, Iron continued, I'm not frightening and I am not afraid, I am a friend. For an entire hour, the tiger and the human stared into one another's eyes, until the tiger lay down and rolled onto his back.

"The animal trusts me," Iron whispered to Carlo. "Don't move, don't let anyone get close, our eye contact must not be broken." Iron approached the cage, opened the door, entered, and locked the door behind him. Carlo and the guard tensed. Iron went to the tiger and scratched him on his belly. The huge predator purred in pleasure. The female, who all this time had been waiting in the corner of the cage, got close to the male and to the human who turned his gaze toward her. She rubbed her back against him. After long minutes, Iron got up and looked at the animals. They retreated to a corner of the cage. Iron sat on a bench in the middle of the cage, looked again into the eyes of the male and signaled over his head with his hand. To Carlo's amazement, the animal stood up and looked like he intended to pounce. "Don't move, and don't dare interfere!" Iron called.

The guard watched the tiger with dread as it vaulted over Iron's head. The female tiger leapt after him. After a few minutes, Iron left the cage with a wide smile.

"I almost forgot how much fun the circus is. There's nothing like making a connection with such a powerful animal, with a soul that is so… childish." During Iron's entire life in the circus, he had never encountered an animal like this.

"What did you do in there?" Carlo asked, his voice shaking.

"I spoke to them. If only I could teach you to do it, but it's a skill you can only acquire when young; afterwards, it's too late." In that moment, Iron made three new fans: two Bengal tigers and one Italian circus manager.

## 2

After Carlo's birth, his mother refused to continue performing in the circus and left with the infant. The mocking fates lay in wait for her in the suburbs of Milan in the form of a virulent tuberculosis bacterium. Carlo's father took care of her through the last weeks of her life and brought Carlo back to the circus with him.

From the age of five, Carlos learned all the circus professions, from cleaning cages to taking care of the animals, clowning, acrobatics, and juggling with three, four, even five balls. He knew how to walk a tightrope blindfolded, to play the trumpet and the tuba, he also knew how to sing. He learned to fly between the trapeze artists whose job it was to catch and release him at the right moment – but he never returned to the trapeze, not even once, after the incident.

Thirty years had passed since then, and he remembered every minute of it. During the first matinee, the catcher was late to catch his father's right hand by a tenth of a second. The whole circus held its breath while his father hung by his left hand from the hand of the catcher. He clung to that hand and tried to pull himself up. "There has never been and never will be a net under me!" he always said with pride. "People pay to see me in danger – not to see me fall pleasantly into a net."

He remembered himself, a young man barely eighteen, watching in horror as his father hung between earth and sky. The whole matter took a minute, maybe less. Sergio, the clown, was the first to get a hold of himself. He ran to one of the cranes, released the rope that tied the trapeze and pulled it down. But to young Carlo it felt like forever. When his father's feet touched the ground, Carlo ran to him in tears. His father pushed him away, strode to the middle of the stage and bowed to the audience. At the end of the performance, he called to his son and said, "Remember to bow to the audience. Even if something unexpected happens, the audience must believe that it was supposed to happen that way." Carlo never forgot those words.

During the performance that took place that same night, despite the pleading from his friends and the manager of the circus, his father climbed the ladder, mounted the trapeze, warmed himself up swinging, once, twice, sat for another swing or two, and then caught the bar with his hands. The bar slipped from his wounded hand, and he fell, hitting the ground with a powerful blow. Carlo caught sight of his eyes staring into space and then he was immediately taken away on a stretcher. The clowns quickly took the stage, Carlo among them. That's the way of the world. The show must go on.

Carlo refused to eat or drink. He lay in his wagon, the image of his father returning to his mind. After two days, the door of the cabin opened and standing in the doorway was the circus manager.

"Good evening, Carlo. Look at me when I talk to you."

Carlo turned his head and stared at the circus manager, his eyes red from crying and lack of sleep. "Yes, Maestro."

"We lost your father - a dear man, a good friend, and one of the greatest circus artists we knew. It is my responsibility to bury him, and I will not do it without you." Carlo stood and crossed the wagon toward the door. "Show a little respect. Wash yourself, dress nicely, comb your hair. Your father deserves at least that from his only son."

During the funeral service, Carlo eulogized his father and, afterwards, participated in a festive meal saturated with alcohol in which the whole circus, each in his own way, said goodbye to his friend and colleague.

For about twenty hours a day, the manager kept Carlo busy with training, rehearsals, and shows. He made him responsible for maintaining the tent and wagons. "Your knowledge of the circus professions is excellent. Now, I want you to learn the secrets of management," he said.

"Why?" asked the exhausted youth. "I don't want to stay with the circus." The manager smiled. "I'll teach you. If you want to leave – leave. We'll start with arithmetic. You can't manage without knowing arithmetic. I understand Gertrude taught you to read Italian, German, and a little English, right?"

"Yes."

"Wonderful. Now I will teach you the rest, everything you need to know to manage a circus."

For almost seven years, the manager educated Carlo. He taught him accounting, how to arrange shows in different locations and in other countries, how to fold up the circus and transport it at minimum expense. He taught him how to hire artists at the beginning of their careers and how to sell them for a lot of money after promoting them and, of course, how to create a fascinating show and tailor it to the local audience. There was one thing the owner insisted on – a ring master's podium. "From there, you can best feel the heartbeat of the circus," he said.

But the most important lesson of all, he taught Carlo during World War I and the difficult period that followed, a lesson that prepared him to survive and keep the circus alive through the Second World War, as well, right until the end. Almost.

In his twenties, Carlo began to manage the circus. Two years later, the previous circus manager, tired of the nomadic world, moved to Lucca in Tuscany, where Carlo sent most of the profits each month. When he died several years later, the childless manager bequeathed all his property to Carlo; in other words, the circus and his house in Tuscany now belonged to Carlo.

But it was Iron, who appeared as if out of nowhere, a man who knew how to speak to animals, and in whose hands the owner placed the circus that had saved him.

"The clown, Anonymous, wants to hold rehearsals," Iron said, interrupting Carlo's wandering thoughts.

Carlo faced a problem that was new to him: the opening performance of the revamped circus was approaching, and although it was well-formed and good enough, even by the tenth rehearsal, the clowns did not meet his expectations. "From time to time, you can drop any part of the circus," the deceased manager taught him, "But not the clowns. Without clowns, there is no circus."

## 3

While Max knew how to be funny, the mix with the troop of clowns was a failure. "No, no, no!" his angry voice could be heard from the ring. "You're acting like you're enjoying the piece, not like your lives depend on the audience laughing…"

The clowns looked at him in amazement. "It's a circus, we're clowns, not gladiators. Our job it to make people laugh, not to fight until someone gives us a thumbs-up," said the oldest of the clowns, speaking for them all.

Alexandra's entrance to the ring lowered the tension a little.

Max approached her. "They don't understand what I want from them…" he said impatiently.

"They grew up in the circus, and you on the stage. Why don't you appear in an independent piece of your own?"

The silence that fell over the tent was broken by Carlo's applause.

Alexandra studied the gloomy smile on Max's face and asked herself if it really was the right way to go. Despite her concern, the reactions of her partners and the other clowns left no doubt: the last piece of the puzzle had fallen into place. Now there was only one thing left.

"What will the circus be called?" asked Carlo.

"Dantes," said Max, "Circus Dantes," and chills ran up Alexandra's spine.

# 4

Aishé felt more frustrated than ever. For someone who had been used to living in nature and always on the move, the apartment was a kind of prison, and Iron was almost never there. He divided his time between managing Alexandra's businesses and taking care of Thomas; he also dedicated a significant portion to the circus - and to Aishé's sorrow - to training the animals. She understood that this work kept them comfortably supported and -more significantly - that Alexandra and Iron's lives were intertwined with Thomas', who was like a son to Iron.

In her own, smart way, Aishé found her way into Thomas' heart and occasionally invited him to visit her in the apartment. There, she sat with him for long stretches. He taught her to read and write, corrected her spoken language, and she would laugh and repeat the correct pronunciation after him. She loved him and enjoyed doing her part, which also lightened Iron's days and endeared her to Alexandra. But she was still lonely.

"Where are you coming from, so late?"

Iron pressed his mouth against hers and kissed her for a long time. "My Aishé, you have nothing to worry about, I love you. The circus…"

"Again, the circus. All the time I hear from you only about the circus and the big cats."

"There's a lot of work. I have to make sure everything is managed properly, and…" Her heart skipped a beat. She was used to the good-hearted giant not hesitating when he answered. "And what?" she asked, her anger diluted with worry.

"I love you, my silly girl, love I never experienced before you, but… Alexandra and Thomas are my family. It all started with two kittens," said Iron, and went on to tell her about how he met Franz and, through him, met Alexandra and Thomas, and how his life was changed.

While lying awake at night, Aishé realized that her situation would only get worse when the circus travelled, and then she wouldn't see her beloved for months. A powerful desire to take part in the circus was awakened.

In the middle of the night, she woke Iron and asked to see the palm of his hand. Iron immediately opened his hand for her. Aishé gently pet his large, open palm with her finger, and gazed at it for a long time. "I see a great love," she said. "I see a boy, wait, two children, a big boy... like his father.... and a little girl belonging to... a fortune teller." She continued to study the giant palm. "The fortune teller... she will work in a circus... she will make you a girl so beautiful, like the sun and moon together."

Iron pulled his hand away excitedly. "And I drove myself crazy trying to figure out what I would do when the circus leaves for distant lands, and what would happen if Alexandra and Max and Thomas wanted me to go with them, and what..." He stopped a moment and took a deep breath. "Yes, Aishé, of course, you'll come with me and read the fortunes of everyone who comes to see the circus. We'll set up a tent just for you, people will pay extra to hear your wisdom. That way you will be close to me, and to Thomas and Alexandra. We will be a circus family, at least until the big boy and beautiful girl you see in my future are born.

# 5

Although Alexandra was reunited with the man who had been the first and only love of her life, sometimes she missed her life with Franz. A simple, cultured life that didn't demand that she solve problems, manage businesses, or resolve conflicts and arguments. More than once, she asked herself if she had made a mistake by agreeing to fulfill her beloved's crazy wishes. Despite her love and commitment to him, her doubts grew. Alexandra drew strength from the positive moments and events that occurred in her life, like the article that appeared in the German newspaper about the personal diary of the former Gestapo commander of Bavaria that was now in the hands of the Americans. It read, "Dozens of SS and Gestapo officers have been caught and are being brought to justice for the war crimes they committed." Alexandra and Iron both paused in the race of living for a moment and remembered the man who had been benevolent to them.

# 1936, Berlin

## 1

Franz left his office and strode to his car. Next to the door of the car, Iron waited for him in a sparkling uniform and with a wide smile. "Good evening, Commander," he said and opened the door while bowing deeply. Franz smiled back at him. He couldn't believe the change that had taken place in him in the span of two months. It wasn't only the uniform that fit his body so perfectly, but that Iron already spoke the language nearly perfectly. He had known that his secretary, Suzanna, the serious, older, single woman, would adopt the giant man with the heart of a babe, and take him to her heart, and so it was. She took him under her wing and taught him, as if he were a toddler, how to eat and how to behave in society, to speak proper German, and even to read and write. Iron was a talented student, there was no doubt about it. Suzanna thought maybe her love would be a tonic for his miserable life, and maybe it was because of her that Iron was so committed to his studies.

Franz knew how to choose people that were right for him and who would meet his needs. He also made sure they would get along well with one another. He was very pleased with Iron's service. Iron woke up early each morning, went down to Suzanna's apartment and returned to pick up Franz a quarter of an hour before the set time. He always started the car in time to pick Franz up at the office as scheduled and warm up the passenger seat beforehand. Franz wondered how Iron knew exactly what time to do each thing. Interesting what he knows about me and doesn't say, he thought.

"Home?" asked Iron.

"Yes, just stop next to Berger's book shop on the way, please."

Iron slid into first gear, released the clutch, and the black Mercedes moved silently forward. Franz was again amazed by the gentleness with which his wide feet handled the different pedals. He himself never learned to drive and had no sense of what it required. Iron stopped next to the store, and Franz got out of the car and disappeared inside. Iron waited for him in the running car. He knew his commander would spend the whole night reading a thick book that he bought today and would finish in another day or so. He wondered why his commander wasn't married or friendly with women. While he was busy with these thoughts, his nose caught the sour smell of fear. From the time he ran barefoot through the streets of Budapest like a wild animal, he had learned to recognize the smell which was similar to the smell of sweat. He recognized the source as three men standing in front of Berger's picture window, looking at the books on display.

Iron got out of the car and slowly closed the distance between himself and the threesome. Despite the appearance of calm, his senses were primed for what was about to happen. The hair on the back of his neck stood on end. His heartrate increased. His vision shrank in focus.

It all happened in an instant. Franz came out of the store with a book in hand, the three pulled out knives and lunged for him, and Iron galloped forward. He grabbed the coat collar of the one closest, threw him to the floor and stomped on his neck. Franz heard the snap of his neck break. The second attacker succeeded in reaching Franz and wounding his chest, but Iron caught him and threw him against his friend's head. "I want them alive!" Franz cried before he lost consciousness.

## 2

Franz opened his eyes in a strange white room on an unfamiliar bed.

"Where am I?" he asked, and immediately a gentle hand rested on his shoulder. He turned his head and saw a nurse in her white uniform.

"You're in the military hospital in Berlin," she said softly. "You were wounded, but it's just a small cut. Doctor Wolf sutured it. I'll call him."

"Iron, call Iron."

"That's his name? I thought he was joking."

There was no need to call Iron. The minute he heard the voice of the commander, he hurried to his bedside.

"Iron so sorry. Iron not guard good his commander. You almost to die, and I smell the bastards. I do know something not good to happen."

"You saved my life, Iron. Thank you, you could not have reacted more quickly."

"I go back to street. Too good life with Commander and Suzanna, make Iron slow and weak. Iron not protect his commander good."

"Shut up!" Franz raised his voice as much as he could. "You did the best you could, and I am grateful to you! I will not hear another word of apology, you understand? You signed a draft agreement with the Gestapo, and you will remain in the Gestapo until I release you, or die, understood?"

"Yes, Commander," whispered Iron.

"Excellent. What condition is the threesome in? I will want to interrogate them."

"The first died, forbidden to leave a person alive behind my back. The two others live like you tell me. After you interrogate, I kill them?"

Franz smiled at Iron's last words. Once Iron understood his commander wasn't angry with him, he returned to himself and the proper German Suzanna had taught him. The afternoon's events proved how right Franz had been to choose Iron as a bodyguard. Without him, he surely would have died.

Dr. Wolf asked to admit Franz for at least a few days, but Franz refused. "I must quickly interrogate and learn who wanted to murder a Gestapo commander and why."

They agreed that he would spend the night at the hospital and be released in the morning.

Suzanna entered the room, as cool and efficient as ever. She asked Franz how he was, congratulated Iron on his success, and within minutes updated Franz with the names of the assassins, SS men all three, friends of Gerd Miller, who Iron had killed, along with his friend, two months earlier. Franz dictated an explanation to Suzanna that tied them to an SS cell, led by Gerd Miller, that was plotting to murder the Führer with the help of the Jewish underground. "Gerd Miller and his friend," he dictated, "were caught and killed by my personal assistant, Untersharführer Iron Mensch. The last attackers wanted to avenge his death. One of them was killed, and the two others confessed. It is my opinion that the cell has been completely eradicated, and there is no need to continue the investigation. I await instructions whether to investigate the matter further. Heil Hitler."

Franz knew the letter of congratulations he received from Himmler after eliminating the "underground" and catching its leader Max Fischer, was not warmly received by many of the senior SS members in Berlin, and he worried that the additional power he had amassed could now work against him. Therefore, he willingly accepted an appointment to the post of Gestapo Commander of Bavaria before someone started snooping around his past and discovered it was a Jew who supported his studies and lived with his mother to this day.

# 1942, Gestapo Headquarters, Munich

## 1

"Something's bothering you, boss. Something in your animal inside that you call a soul doesn't make sense to me," Iron said as they ate breakfast together. Franz looked into Iron's eyes again, this time taking a longer look. He hoped Iron would see the answer in his eyes, and he wouldn't have to say the words himself, the truth that he was part of this big machine that located Jews and sent them to their death.

"I am forced to do things I completely disagree with," he said finally. "Which will lead, ultimately, to the destruction of Germany." Franz paused and took a deep breath. "You know I was drafted into the Gestapo because of my expertise as a detective. I swore then to obey the rules of the country, but who knew that instead of chasing criminals, we would chase Jews because of their religion? That I would recruit Jews to rat out other Jews?"

"So why don't you leave?"

"Enough, Iron, you're not simple-minded. How many days or hours will I survive if I don't sit in this seat? You know how many enemies I've made?" He signaled Iron not to interrupt him. "Even you will not be able to save me from the harsh hand of the SS or the Gestapo. It will be my end. My life depends on how many people are afraid of me and the information I have about their lives."

"What kind of information, for example, could frighten an officer of the SS?"

"A Jewish grandmother or lover, homosexuality, money stolen from the Reich and transferred to Switzerland, membership in the communist party while in school... I collect it all, write it all down, store it all here, too," Franz said pointing at his head. "Please ask Suzanna to make me a cup of tea. I must work." He didn't bother specifying how much sugar.

Iron left Franz's office and looked at the older woman who was the closest thing to a mother he had ever known. "I know everything about him," she answered when Iron asked about the sugar. "How he likes his tea and when, what he eats at every meal, which books he likes to read. I buy him his food, his clothes, his shoes... I know what kind of toothpaste he prefers, although with the war these days, it's very hard to get a hold of English-made toothpaste and shaving cream. But you, who are like a son to me, about you I don't know enough. For example, I don't know why you were thrown out of the circus."

"Franz asked for tea. Make him a cup and I will tell you everything," said Iron.

Suzanna fulfilled Franz's request and sat across from Iron. "Our boss is in a terrible mood," she said.

"I know. We should leave him be. And now we have about an hour. I will tell you what I have never told a soul, why I was thrown out of the circus."

"I'm very curious to hear."

"I very much enjoyed life in the circus," Iron began. "It's also where I learned about women. I had an easy time with women," he said. "I know what they want, and what they mean. They think completely differently from how we men do. I knew how to make them look at me with eyes in heat."

"Oy, stop, you're embarrassing me. Speak in clean language, please."

"Forgive me, Suzanna, I see you're embarrassed, but I have no other way to explain it. I saw a look like this among animals in heat, but a woman can have that look not only when she is in heat."

"Fine, fine, but why did they throw you out of the circus?"

"Because of that. My success with women annoyed many of the men in the circus. And worst of all, there were women who were angry that I had relations with other women…" Iron looked in her eyes. "Why do women confuse love with lust, Suzanna?"

"I'm not a big expert in the field," she said and avoided his penetrating gaze.

"With the other men, I got along, because they were afraid of me, but when the daughter of the circus manager asked if I loved her just after we slept together, and I answered that I desire her, her father threw me out of the circus."

"And then?"

"That's it, I started living on the streets of Berlin and made a living in shows of strength or boxing with gypsy bears, until I met two kittens that the SS men…"

"Yes, I know the rest," she said. "Now give me a hug, you overgrown gorilla."

Iron lifted the small woman to his chest and hugged her with the love he would have felt for his mother, if he had had a mother.

"Our boss is in a terrible mood," she said again when her breath returned. "Maybe take him out to the cabaret or some nightclub, so he'll meet some people who aren't investigators or people being investigated? Maybe… maybe even help him meet a woman?"

"Do you know how many women I've introduced to him? Women who were ready to get into his bed in a minute... You know that uniforms drive women crazy?

"Enough, stop," Suzanna grumbled. "Go on, and he wasn't interested?"

"He recoiled from them, it's as if he's afraid of women," Iron said. "A man so strong and smart, and afraid of a woman. I don't understand it." He shook his head. "What did you say? Cabaret? Not a bad idea. I'm also up for a cabaret..."

"Iron, 'I'm also up' is not German, it's foul language you picked up on the street here in Bavaria. Say, "I'd like," or more casually, I'm in the mood for, is that clear?" Iron again gathered her up in his arms and lifted her in the air.

"Leave me be, you're smushing me," Suzanna said, but she reveled in the pampering.

"Surely you meant to say, "These are my bones you are crushing..." answered Iron, imitating her syntax.

That same day on their way home, Iron told his commander about a cabaret where the hottest star in Munich had been singing for a long time, under the moniker, 'the Baroness.' He suggested they go there together. After many years of working with Iron, and Iron assisting him more than once at getting to the truth during complex investigations, he knew his soul and understood his heart. Franz realized that he himself would never crack the soul of his loyal assistant. He acquiesced to his request to visit the Red Lantern nightclub.

# 2

As was his way, Franz wore civilian clothes. He was repulsed by the false display of respect given him or his uniform by waiters in restaurants and even people on the street. But Suzanna made sure he would get the best possible service and informed the manager of the nightclub ahead of time, that the Gestapo Commander of Bavaria would honor them with his presence. "Please do not address him by name or title, and do not mention his presence over the loudspeakers," she said.

About an hour before the scheduled show, Franz and Iron arrived at the club, Iron also in civilian clothes, and they received the best table in the house, right in front of the stage. A bottle of French champagne was pulled out ceremoniously and placed on their table in a silver ice bucket.

"On the house," said the excited waiter, who knew only that before him sat an important man in Germany.

Iron poured champagne into the glasses and raised his glass, "To your life, my Commander. Without you, I would have been smelling the flowers from below a long time ago," he smiled as he delivered the toast he had learned in the circus. "Commander, please let loose a little," he added.

Franz tasted the champagne with pleasure and smiled.

At the end of the opening acts that didn't interest Franz at all, the MC got on stage and announced in an excited voice, "Ladies and gentlemen, I'm proud to present the most talented singer in Munich, a singer who will make you laugh and cry, please welcome the one and only, the most beautiful and talented of them all, welcome…" The drumroll started and grew in power, and the MC called at the top of his lungs, "the Baroness!" The drums fell silent, the curtain parted, and Alexandra, in her long, sparkling, red dress with the wide, plunging neckline and the slit up her right thigh – burst onto the stage. Her entrance was so spectacular, the audience went dumb. The Baroness wrapped her hands around the microphone and said in a low voice, "Good evening to you, too!" Her greeting was answered with ringing applause. She lifted her hand and the audience fell silent again. "This is a special day for me, it's my dear mother's birthday, I ask you all to raise a glass in her honor."

"A known trick to increase the amount of drinking," Iron whispered to his commander.

"Every one of you has someone you love who might be celebrating something, think about them, about your dear ones, about those fighting now for Germany and about those at home, or maybe here, right next to you – Prost!" The audience responded enthusiastically, and she sang a familiar birthday song. When it ended, the orchestra played a rousing military song, which she executed lightly with the addition of a drunken dance.

Iron melted with pleasure. Suddenly, he recognized a spark in his commander's eye similar to the one he saw when Franz was completely focused on a new and interesting case.

### 3

From the moment Alexandra got on stage, Franz's breath caught. On stage was Alexandra Brecholdt. His brain refused to believe his eyes. It did not make sense that the best of the German actresses would appear in this kind of hovel, in Munich... But what his eyes saw and his ears heard – his brain could not deny. It was her in all her glory, Alexandra Brecholdt. And here, of all places, is where Iron had dragged him. He wondered if Iron knew what he was doing, if he planned it ahead of time, if he had sensed on some other occasion, the turmoil she would cause him.

"She's good, the singer," Iron interrupted his thoughts. He looked at Iron and answered, "Better than good." Iron understood that Franz was referring to more than her singing.

Suddenly, Franz said, in a tone that didn't invite questions, "Take me to the office." Iron stood immediately. "Yes, Commander."

Disappointed and confused, Iron drove Franz to the Gestapo command.

"You can go home to sleep; I'll spend the night here. Please come tomorrow with a clean uniform for me," Franz continued to surprise him.

Iron left the command without another word and drove to a large apartment where an attractive woman was living. She was lonely and worried about the fate of her husband, a decorated officer in the German air force. The rest of the night turned into a long party in which he forgot about his commander's strange behavior and she, her worries for her husband. When they parted in the wee hours of the morning, the two did not know that with the dawn their worlds would turn upside down. Iron's world – because of the cabaret singer who would change his life; and her world – because of a short and violent aerial encounter between her husband and a determined British pilot who squeezed the trigger on his canon a fraction of a second earlier than her husband squeezed his.

## 4

Franz entered his office, called the on-duty secretary, and dictated the first telegram to his colleague in the central command in Berlin, in which he asked to receive all the information he had about the actress Alexandra Brecholdt. "Please focus on the years between the Führer's rise to power and the start of the war. Stop. Heil Hitler. Stop." He talked to the local Munich police command and asked to know when Alexandra Brecholdt moved to Munich. He also asked the secretary on duty to check with the Gestapo archive if anything had been written about Alexandra. He was determined to clarify every detail about her. Next, he called a reporter involved in local culture and gossip. Franz knew his sexual leanings, but he didn't report them. He knew he would need his services in situations like this, for example.

After the conversation, Franz took off his shoes and put his feet up on his desk. He leaned back, locked eyes with the picture of the Führer hanging on the wall and sank into his thoughts until he fell asleep.

Iron arrived at daybreak the next day and found his commander leaning back in his chair, his feet resting on the desk.

"Commander, I brought you clean clothes…"

Franz opened his eyes and didn't wonder for a moment where he was and why. "Thank you. Leave them here, and ask Suzanna to come in."

"I'm here," Suzanna's voice could be heard just outside the door. "I just got here now."

As he did nearly every morning, Franz started his day with a series of conversations with his various informants. From time to time, he thought about the actress he admired, Alexandra Brecholdt.

He waited for the information about her to arrive from all the sources he had contacted. It will be the gossipy reporter who will bring the goods, he thought.

A ring on his private line interrupted his thoughts.

"Franz Schmidt, Heil Hitler," he answered sharply. There were only a few people who had access to this phone line. The name of the game, for the time being, was to be very careful.

"It's me." And, indeed, it was the reporter who got back to him first.

"Talk to me."

"It's an interesting story. I knew about it, of course; I just confirmed some small details."

"My time is limited, get to the point."

"Frau Brecholdt's marriage to Baron Claus von Basarab was a marriage of convenience, meant to hide the fact that he is a homosexual."

Franz worked to hide his surprise. "Are you sure?"

"Personal knowledge," answered the informer, his wide grin audible over the telephone line.

"Continue."

"The baby was born about seven and a half months after the wedding, weighing in at three and a half kilos. I checked with the midwife."

"Very nice."

"And then he ran off with some pretty face who came from England hunting a nobleman."

"And she was left with the baby. What about the Baron's father, he has no interest in his grandson?"

"There's no connection between them. It's not clear why."

"Anything else?"

"Yes, she sings at the Red Lantern club, earning a living from the shows. And what is your interest in her, Commander?"

"You stick your nose in your own business and in what I tell you to stick it in, is that clear?"

"Yes, Commander. My apologies, Commander."

"Good work, thank you," Franz sweetened his answer. He finished the conversation and wrote down in his notebook: Marriage to a homosexual, reasonable to assume she knew as much before the wedding. Married quickly because she was pregnant? By him? To hide his sexual inclination? How did that serve her? What was she hiding?

He asked Suzanna to send the reporter a bottle of French wine.

From Berlin, a telegram arrived stating that Alexandra Brecholdt was suspected by the SS of a romantic connection with the Jewish theater actor, Max Fischer, but undercover agents tracking her could not prove the existence of the relationship. The tail came to a stop after the actor was arrested, her marriage ended, and her move to Munich. Franz wrote in his notebook, "An affair with Max Fischer? Is there a connection to the wedding?" He put the notebook in the drawer, closed it, and called Iron.

"Take me home," he said. "I need some sleep. Tonight, we'll go back to the Red Lantern."

# 5

At exactly the same time, Alexandra awoke from her afternoon nap. She looked at her watch. She had to hurry to take Thomas home from school. At night, she would take him with her. The nanny who helped her had informed her she wouldn't be able to watch him that night. It happened more than once, but Alexandra knew she had to earn a living, and her work met their needs. She was a single mother in a foreign city, renting an apartment, paying a nanny, and taking care of food and clothing. What remained of her salary, in the months when there was anything left, she sent to her mother in Berlin. She loved her work and made peace with the fact that she had to take advantage of her femininity and her acting ability to tempt men into buying her drinks at absurd prices. It was a significant part of her salary, and she needed it.

# 1945, Munich, Circus Dantes

## 1

The worry that not enough people would come to see the circus dissipated hours before the opening of their first show. The audience crowded the exits, and Carlo ran between the artists, the technical crew, the animal cages, and the ticket booth. As a boy who had grown up in the circus, he knew the experience the children have outside the tent sometimes supersedes the one inside the show, and therefore he opened the gates to the public.

The time of the performance grew closer. He signaled to the trumpeters to trumpet loudly, donned his top hat and red coat, and climbed up to the ring master's podium. The orchestra broke into fast-paced, loud music.

"Ladies and gentlemen, boys and girls, mothers and fathers, I'm happy to see all of you here at the premiere performance of Circus Dantes! Please welcome the artists!"

The orchestra played a cheerful march, and Claude de Button entered the ring. He walked with light steps and looked like he was whistling casually for his own pleasure. When he arrived at the center of the ring, he stopped, turned around, and gestured to signal his friends to join him, but no one came. Claude turned to look at Carlo and raised his arms in wonder – what should he do?

"Pull them, Claude, they got stuck in the mud," Carlo roared. Claude pulled hard on an imaginary rope accompanied by the sounds of cymbals. When he got tired, he stopped. But the cymbals continued to make noise. Without them, there would have been complete silence in the giant tent.

"Pull Claude, pull! Children, help Claude! Clap your hands!"

Carlo started applauding rhythmically, and the audience joined him.

"Pull, Claude, pull!" he cried. "Pull, Claude, pull!" the voices of the children in the audience called loudly. Claude seemed to be encouraged and pulled. He pulled more and more quickly on the invisible rope. First a clown with cymbals burst into the ring, then jugglers juggling balls, clubs, and even flaming torches. Claude stopped, pulled an invisible handkerchief from his invisible pocket, and wiped the invisible sweat from his brow. The parade stopped the orchestra grew silent. "Pull, Claude, pull," screamed the children.

Claude tossed the rope over his shoulder and continued to pull the parade. As they exited the ring, white horses appeared with sculpted women daringly dressed positioned on their backs. The young women waved their arms in the air in greeting.

## 2

Backstage, Alex, Iron, and Max watched the action. While the first two enjoyed the original opening, Max was left tense. "I'll be back in a few minutes," he said, and went to his wagon. No one knew that, at that moment, the laugh thundered in his head, loud and clear and horrifying.

Iron was filled with pride. What a good call he had made by appointing Carlo manager of the circus and giving him free reign.

He himself had prepared a special bit for the opening night. A bit like this was sure to wow the audience, who certainly had never experienced anything like it before.

Carlo ran the show with an exacting hand. He brought Claude back for additional bits and, while he performed his amazing pantomime, flying acrobats entered the ring, two men and a woman, and amazed the audience with daring aerial summersaults and jumps. At the same time, the stagehands assembled the cage for the big cats. The orchestra quieted except for a single drum that began a soft drum roll that grew louder and louder. A large man stood inside the cage.

He raised his arm, waited a moment, and then lowered it in a sharp movement. The orchestra fell silent.

Iron whistled a short whistle and in a pleasant voice, called, "Sigmund, why don't you join me, the audience wants to meet you."

A large tiger climbed onto the stage, looked into Iron's eyes, and walked silently towards the cage. Every few steps, he roared and bowed his head as if waiting for applause which indeed did not tarry to come. "Go get Bellissima, we both miss her," Iron said.

The large animal left the cage he had just entered, turned backstage and returned.

"Why isn't she coming? Does she need a special invitation?"

Those who sat closest to the ring, swear to this day that the large animal looked into the man's eyes and nodded.

"Okay, fine. Bellissima, this show is not a show without you, please join us!"

The large female trotted out onto the stage, headed straight for Iron, put her paws on Iron's shoulders and brought her head close to his face. The audience roared in fear. The guards who stood outside the cage tensed, but all the worry and fear were for naught. The tigress rubbed her nose against Iron's nose, until Iron pulled away from her. "You promised me you wouldn't eat onions before the show," he said, and she retreated to her corner, as if insulted.

Iron continued to amaze the audience. He put his head into the tiger's jaw and sat on the floor of the cage while the two terrifying animals leapt over his head back and forth, but he saved the best for last.

"Come, child," he cried. "Yes, you." He pointed towards a child sitting in the first row.

From her position backstage, Alexandra was surprised to see her son take his place inside the cage before the jaws of this terrifying, wild animal. Thomas reached out with his finger and the tiger drew close to him and scratched his nose with the outstretched finger. Neither Thomas nor Iron noticed Bellissima sneak up behind them, reaching her paw out to Thomas' shoulder and knocking him onto his back. Alexandra screamed in shock along with the audience. Iron reached out to pull her back, but to everyone's surprise, Bellissima sat down and licked Thomas' face with her rough tongue.

While the audience applauded excitedly, a drama took place behind the scenes that is hard to describe in words.

"How dare you endanger the life of my son!" Alexandra beat on Iron's chest as he left the ring. She released her fury and then burst into tears. Aishé approached her and gave her a long hug. She threw a disparaging look at Iron.

"Alexandra, you know I would never endanger Thomas, he's... like my own child..."

Max emerged from his wagon and hugged Alexandra, and then he placed a hand on Thomas' shoulder and asked, "What did you feel on stage?"

"It was wonderful, Papa, the audience applauded and... and...

and Sigmund was cute, he wanted some attention and I scratched him on the nose… but then Bellissima came…"

"Look how he enjoyed himself and knows what he's doing. He's a natural talent, your son, he's born for this life. And you, Thomas," he looked at the boy and waved his finger at him to emphasize his words, "Call me Max, okay?"

Thomas nodded, and Alexandra looked at Max angrily. "That is the last time he enters the lion cage!" she yelled.

## 3

**"I have set before you life and death… choose life."**
(Deuteronomy, 30:19)

Max barely slept that night. About two hours after he fell asleep, he was awakened by the laugh, stronger and louder than ever. Every time he closed his eyes, images flashed in his head. Each member of his family who he had not remembered returned and was revealed before his closed eyes. Here was his mother smiling, conciliatory, calming. There was not a person in the world who held a grudge against her. He wanted to apologize for sometimes having raised his voice to her. He wanted to embrace her, kiss her, take refuge in her familiar scent, and now she was replaced by the figure of his father, aristocratic and stubborn. "Papa, don't go, wait!" he screamed. The Passover table appeared, his whole family seated around it, David seated in his highchair, his thumb in his mouth and his face beaming. When was that, yesterday? An eternity ago? And again, he could not hold on to the image. Then his father-in-law, arguing fervently about the danger threatening the Jews in Germany, appeared before him. "May God make you like Ephraim and Menashe... May God bless you and keep you..." his father whispered and rested his hands over his head, and here is Bertha, his wife, on the street, pushing David's baby carriage. On this night, he remembered them all, and on this night, he parted from all whom he had loved. The act of parting is always agonizing but, while Max was aware that his entire family had been murdered, he had never said goodbye to them until now, as he could not conjure them in his imagination. Only on this night did he truly experience being torn from them, with all its devastating force. Memories of his happy life battered him like a hurricane – memories of the life he'd had and was no longer. For a moment, he considered taking a razor and cutting his veins to join the world he had lost, but he immediately fell back into a fevered sleep. This time his wife, Bertha, came to him and whispered in his ear, "You have love and you have a purpose, Max, your time is not over, fulfill your purpose. Don't let death and evil vanquish you, as well." Max tried to open his eyes and ask her about his purpose, but she waved goodbye and dissolved in the night air.

In the early afternoon of the following day, he got out of bed, got dressed and shaved his beard with the same razorblade he had considered using to take his life, just several hours earlier. The mirror before him reflected a man more determined than ever.

# 1946, Circus Dantes

After months of successful shows in Munich, the circus' reputation had spread far and wide. The circus hands pulled up the stakes and dismantled the tent and headed out towards other cities in Germany. The audience was smitten by the wonders of the circus and by Alexandra's charm. She had become popular during evening performances, so popular that sometimes Carlo brought her back on stage to sing even more songs.

During the show, Max watched the audience and its reactions. He was pleased that his ability to predict them improved from show to show. But he still avoided performing himself. "The mad laugh that echoes in my ears makes it impossible for me to focus," he made excuses to Alexandra.

Instead of holding rehearsals and preparing his clowning performance, Max spent quite a bit of time with the acrobats and began to practice with them. In the beginning, he worked with the help of simple aids on the ground. As his body got stronger, he was drawn more and more to the aerial acrobatics taking place just below the ceiling of the circus tent. He learned to walk a tightrope, to swing on the trapeze, and even to jump from one swing to another and then passed from thrower to catcher.

One day, Alexandra entered the ring and the situation got

complicated. At the exact moment when Max let go of the trapeze and did a layout; he reached for the catcher, but missed. He fell to the safety net below him and, like an experienced acrobat, he jumped off the net and stood on the ground smiling.

"What do you think you're doing?" Alexandra asked quietly, despite the flash in her eyes.

"Giovanni and I are practicing layouts," Max answered calmly.

"We have something to talk about, Max. Can you come with me, please?"

"Just a minute, we…"

"Now!"

Alexandra had never spoken to him in that tone before. She strode quickly towards the wagons, and he, after her. "Not for this did I establish a circus, so you can fall and die before my eyes!" she said and locked the door behind them.

"I'm just practicing, there's a net underneath, Carlo makes sure of it… the acrobatics strengthens my body, my focus, my balance. I'll need all that to fulfill my true calling – to be a clown as I was meant to be."

Alexandra glared at him angrily. "Do you even know who 'meant' for you to be clown? Who decided that clowning is your true calling?"

"What are you trying to tell me, Alex? What do you mean, 'who decided?'"

Alexandra remained silent.

"I'm begging you, Alex, tell me, I must know."

Maybe it was the sad, pleading look in his eyes that made her say what she said, maybe it was the sense of fracture that she had been feeling for some time. Yes, she had gotten Max back, but her family had not been reunited. She did not have back the Max she had known and who now hid behind this broken man, nor did she get back a father for Thomas. And she knew who caused this break.

"It was Kurt Decker. He decided you would be a clown."

She approached Max to hug him, but Max stopped her and looked into her eyes. His pupils widened. He opened his mouth to scream but choked it back with his fists. His face twisted and tears streamed down his cheeks. That is how he sat for another long hour. "Yes, Kurt Decker. Thank you for keeping that secret all these years. Thank you for not telling me earlier and thank you even more for telling me now. Right, I remember now, it was Kurt Decker."

She gathered him up into her arms and hugged him hard.

# 1940, Kaufering, Bavaria

## 1

From the moment he was caught by the SS, Max's life passed before his eyes in slow motion, as if in a dream. During the long hours that he sat in the foul-smelling barracks of the camp, he remembered the investigation, the quick sentencing, the long years he spent in the prison in Berlin, the truck onto which he was loaded with other prisoners for the long journey to the camp. He also remembered that he met with his wife and his son, David, but not what had happened during that meeting which ended with the cursed moment in which the officer pulled his son and wife from him. Max remembered David's heart-wrenching cry, a cry that faded as the distance between them grew. He spent more than three years in prison, but he asked to forget every moment of that time. His intense yearning for his son created a power to conjure up his son's face. Here he is at three, running through green fields; he's four and already expressing his opinions. Max imagined him stomping his feet; five and already learning to read and write. He didn't only dream about his son. There was also Alexandra, the actress, who returned his love and occupied his thoughts. Now it seemed like it was all part of another world. And that was a good thing.

Max and many others were pushed out of the truck that had

brought them to the years of imprisonment in the labor camp for enemies of the state in Kaufering, Bavaria. They stood at attention in the wide plaza of the entrance and waited that way for a full hour until the commander of the camp strode out of his office towards the plaza. Max looked at the SS officer, at his pressed uniform and his shiny boots. He looked familiar. The commander delivered a short speech about how the camp was run and detailed the multitude of punishments one could expect if they did not behave accordingly. Almost every sentence ended with, "shot to death," or "hung from a rope." In order to emphasize the seriousness of his intention, the commander signaled to one of his assistants who brought a Gypsy dressed in rags to the expanse. "You are accused of sneaking out of your barracks last night, and into the staff kitchen. Do you admit your guilt?" he asked.

"I was hungry, Commander," whispered the Gypsy.

The commander signaled to his assistant to take notes. "Admits his guilt. The punishment: death by hanging." Within just a few moments, a rope was wrapped around his neck, tightened, and then pulled aloft. The gypsy kicked and fluttered for a long time until he ceased to kick. The rope was released, and the camp commander exploded in wild and violent laughter.

The performance horrified Max. But one thing was as clear to him as day, there was only one man who laughed like that, Kurt Decker, the same Kurt Decker who had been an unsuccessful actor in the Berlin theater.

Kurt didn't miss the amazement on the face of the prisoner who stood third from the right in the second row. As someone who reviewed the lists of new prisoners every day, he well knew that Max Fischer was on his way to the camp, and he had plans for him.

## 2

While his friends in the line-up were released to their barracks, Max was commanded to stand in place. He was frightened but hoped for the best. After all, he and the commander shared the same stage more than once, long before this madness had all begun. Indeed, he was the one who instructed the man in the ways of acting. Max, of course, preferred not to focus on the memory of the fist he planted on the face of the man who had become his jailer, nor on Kurt's crude pursuit of Alexandra. He chose not to remember the destructive power of jealousy that can drive any man out of his wits, in particular, jealousy over a woman; even when the man is a beautiful soul like Othello, and "beautiful soul" is the last thing anyone would choose to call Kurt Decker. Max prayed that Kurt had forgotten the punch. He had still not internalized that, in that crazy time, there was no one in Germany, nor in all of Europe, to listen to anyone's prayers, never mind answer them. Certainly not the prayers of Jews.

"You will be my clown," began Kurt without any words of introduction.

"Clown? What have I to do with clowning, Mr. Decker? You know who I am, I am an actor."

"An actor? Really, Mordechai, you always were and always will be a clown. And you will address me as Commander, is that clear?" Kurt taunted him, addressing him by his Jewish name, the name written in his identification papers that even his parents didn't use.

"Forgive me, sir, but a clown is someone who knows how to make others laugh, with or without a text. I am not a clown at all. I am an empty vessel into whom the playwright delivers content, the translator who does his best to bring the spirit of the original text to his lips. The director interprets the content according to his understanding. I only execute what I am told to do…"

"Finally, I agree with something you said, Mordechai. You had nothing, have nothing, and will have nothing. You are an empty vessel, a prisoner whose whole family has been sent to prison because of your actions against the Third Reich. All the property you exploited from the German people in your greed, was confiscated and you have nothing else of your own!" Kurt erupted in laughter. "You will make me laugh, Mordechai, you will make my guests laugh, you'll learn. I'll teach you better and faster than you taught me to act." Again, the roaring laughter made Max's skin crawl.

Max was sent to the barracks on which hung a sign that read, "Warning. Jews." The door opened and he was assaulted by the stench. Slowly, his eyes adjusted to the darkness, but once he could make out the details before him, it occurred to him that sometimes blindness in the dark is preferable to vision in daylight. Dozens of bunkbeds were crowded into the long barracks. Worn-out men dressed in rags lay or sat on them and stared at the new person who had entered. Some of them prayed, some talked amongst themselves. Someone called, "Hey, fresh meat, come over here, there's an open bed. Yes, I mean you." He approached cautiously. It was a plank on the upper level, covered in a filthy cloth. In the bed next to it, a prisoner was covered with two blankets while Max trembled from cold.

"Hello. I'm Isaac. Yes, you see correctly, when someone dies, someone else immediately takes their blanket; but don't worry, there is order here. Dr. Finkelstein is the doctor and also responsible for the barracks. He will arrange everything right away. In the meantime, it looks to me like you need to rest." Max lay down on the bed and, despite the cold, fell asleep in an instant.

# 3

At nineteen hundred hours, the door of the barracks opened.

"Attention!" Dr. Finkelstein yelled, and immediately everyone stopped what they were doing and sat up. Marching slowly, a guard dressed in an SS uniform entered the barracks. The pressed uniform and shining black boots shone in the darkness. The guard looked around in disgust and read in a loud voice from the slip of paper in his hand, like a merchant selling peaches in the market. "The clown is requested to come immediately." No one in the large barracks moved, including Max, who had just woken up and had only had time to exchange names with those in the neighboring compartments. "I don't like to wait," called the guard, and this time the tone of a casual threat accompanied his voice. "I called the clown." This call too, was met without reaction. The guard looked again at the paper in his hands, "Max Fischer, the clown, come here immediately."

Max was amazed to hear his name emerge from the mouth of the guard, but a gentle push from Isaac brought him back to focus. "I am Max Fischer, but it seems there's been a mistake, I am not a clown," he said as he approached the guard.

"Prisoner number 26546, Max Fischer, Clown. Is that you or not you?" Max was about to answer, but the eyes glaring at him from every direction made it clear, without any words, that it would be best not to argue.

"Yes, sir," said Max and hurried towards the guard. A blow to his neck knocked him face down onto the floor of the barracks. The guard raised his gun for an additional strike, but Max gathered himself and stood, lowering his head in submission as if waiting for the blow while quietly mumbling words of flattery and apology.

If the guard had been a sharp observer, maybe he would have detected that, behind the ingratiating Jew, stood a skilled stage actor. Although the soldier who had once been a merchant in the market had never visited the theater in his life, he stopped the butt of his gun before shattering Max's skull.

Not the guard, nor Max, nor any one of the Jews who silently watched what transpired, knew that the blow Max had been spared was a fateful one. In fact, it would determine the fate of Herschel Leibowitz, who would lose his life several hours later.

The guard pointed at Herschel who was lying on his bunk and signaled him to join them. And thus, the two Jews and the guard strode towards the guards' quarters in the camp.

Max was brought into a large hall, well-lit and well-furnished. To one side, was a richly appointed bar and, on the other, a black grand piano on which an astounding prisoner played Beethoven's Moonlight Sonata. Max immediately recognized the Jewish pianist. About a dozen SS officers celebrated in the hall, alongside a number of men in civilian dress and women in black evening gowns, who dangled on the wrists of the men like jewelry. Waiters in black pants, suit jackets, and white gloves glided among them and served refreshments. The evening was like every other ball at the theater where Max performed so many times in his life, but the worn-out prison garb of the well-known pianist, and the presence of the SS officers, brought him back to the present and the sad farce that had become the reality of his life. That and Kurt Decker, whose thunderous laugh echoed now and then over the voices of his friends and the pleasant sounds of the piano. The pianist finished the sonata and Kurt called out in a big voice, "Ladies, officers, and friends, we have here today a new attraction in your honor, a Jewish clown who will entertain us. Please welcome, Max Fischer the clown!"

Some of those present recognized the name, some had no idea what the theater was, but both those who did and those who didn't, turned their heads toward the direction their host pointed. Max stood embarrassed.

"Let's go, my guests want to laugh!" said Kurt Decker. Max tried to remember the racy jokes his father used to tell beside the dinner table and, to his mother's consternation when she, inevitably, would try to deter him, "Shhh… the children are listening…"

"Once, there was a Jew…" said Max, "who went to synagogue in a foreign town…"

"Max, Max don't repeat the tired jokes we had to listen to and laugh at when you ruled over us… make us laugh, understand?"

"But… I'm an actor," said Max in a weak voice.

"An actor…" Kurt sneered out loud. "A theater actor," he continued when he noticed his audience laughing in enjoyment. "You're not an actor, you're a clown – and you will make us laugh!" He signaled to the guard who brought Herschel Liebowitz from the next room. "I'll teach you how, it's very simple," said Kurt. And he proudly drew his gun from his holster and pressed it against Herschel's temple. "Either you make my guests laugh, or I'll make them laugh my way."

"No, please, no… He didn't do anything! I'll make you laugh."

Max again tried to remember some joke, and this time he told it with a heavy Polish accent and exaggerated movements.

The deafening blast of the shot echoed throughout the enclosed room, and the guests tensed in their seats. Herschel fell and his blood sprayed on the wall behind him. Max's mouth fell open in horror and fainted, and thus he was spared the painful sound of Kurt's crazy laugh, a laugh that infected all those present. Some joined him out of politeness and others because, in their eyes, the performance was, in fact, entertaining. Herschel's body was removed, and three prisoners hurried to clean the fresh blood. Kurt poured a cold beer on Max's face. "You have a week to learn to be funny," he said, "And then we will meet in the same place, at the same time. And remember, if you don't make us laugh, I will!"

Three left the barracks, two Jews and a guard. Only two returned. The third was another prisoner, "shot and killed during an attempt to escape," as was carefully recorded in the camp's administrative records.

Max tossed and turned in his bunk. He studied his friends in the bunk and, without drawing attention to himself, he mimicked their movements. He mimicked the prisoner on the bunk to his right who scratched at the crabs in his groin; the one who woke up from sleep every fifteen minutes and called his wife's name out loud; the one who kept checking if his slice of bread was still hidden under his mattress. I'll make those bastards laugh, I'll make them laugh so they want to see me again and again, I will not break, no matter how long I am here, until Germany is sane again; I will survive. I will find my family and escape with them to America, he thought as he fell asleep. Towards morning, more asleep than awake, he saw in his mind the Little Tramp from Charlie Chaplin's movie, *The Gold Rush*, rolling his shoelaces like spaghetti and eating his shoes – and the Tramp transformed in his imagination from the image of Chaplin to a Jew from the camp.

# 4

"Doctor Finkelstein wishes to meet you," said Isaac to Max when he returned to the barracks in the evening.

"I know who you are," said Dr. Finkelstein. "I saw you in the theater. It's important that I know what you went through last night and why Herschel was killed. We're trying to help our friends survive... but it doesn't always work." He sighed.

Max told him about his meeting with Kurt, about the events of the previous evening, and about Herschel's death. He didn't leave anything out.

"He said a week? We will teach you to be funny," said Dr. Finkelstein. "We will beat these human beasts, these worthless, sadistic, barbarians."

Max sighed. "Is there someone in the barracks who knows how to make all kinds of accessories?" he asked and told Dr. Finkelstein about the idea he had.

"The question is, what can you offer in exchange," answered the doctor.

"There is a lot of food on the tables, I assume that some of it gets thrown away after the party... Maybe I can steal some."

"If that's so, you will be able to save many of those dying from frailty and hunger," said Dr. Finkelstein and called over Zalman and Solomon, a tailor and a shoemaker. He explained to them what was happening and recruited them to prepare a variety of props. The two asked no questions and disappeared between the bunks. Dr. Finkelstein called another individual. "Maybe you've met in the past," he said to them both.

"Max, Max Fischer," cried a skeleton. Despite trying, Max did not recognize him. "I'm Hans Fuchs, have you forgotten me already?"

"Fuchsy!" called Max and smiled. Standing before him was the best make-up artist in the theater. They fell into one another's arms.

"Okay, let's see how you can turn me into the most grotesque Shylock there is," said Max. He didn't have to say more.

Fuchs took a pair of scissors from the doctor and disappeared. He returned with the ends of hair that he cut from the beard of one of the prisoners and improvised glue. He stuck the hair on Max's face to create a tangled beard, and then he painted lines on his face. Max, who had just arrived at the camp, now looked like a prisoner who had lived there his whole life. Solomon and Zalman brought him the phylacteries they made. "We tied a few strips of paper to the *tefillin* so you can eat them without a problem. The *tallis* is also made of paper, you can eat that too." They also brought a tattered coat with wide, deep pockets. "Take care of the coat, we use it for theft," said Solomon.

"Thank you for everything," said Max to the threesome who helped him and to Dr. Finkelstein.

"Yesterday it was Herschel, tomorrow it could be one of us. It's important that you succeed, Max," said the doctor, unwittingly prescient.

## 5

A week later, in the evening, the door of the barracks opened. "Attention!" called Dr. Finkelstein, and they all stood at attention in their places.

"The clown is requested to come at once!" thundered the guard, and Max answered, "I am here, officer, sir."

"You come, too," said the guard and pointed at Dr. Finkelstein.

Everyone present in the barracks held their breaths. Many of them were still alive only because of him. They prayed that if the Divine Will was such that only one of the two men should return, that it would be the doctor and not the clown.

# 6

Max burst into the room with a huge skullcap on his head. He wore the coat that was three sizes too big on him, and his shoes were torn across their fronts. With every step, a scraping flik-flak was heard. The Germans burst into thunderous laughter. After he got tangled in his pants that were too long, and fell flat on his face, he slowly stood up and tried to slide his hands out of the long coat sleeves. In the end, he succeeded, but the moment he lowered his arms to his side, they were again swallowed up by the sleeves. He screamed with fury and repeated the same motions again and again until he sensed that the audience was losing interest. Then he took off the coat, threw it to the ground and jumped on it. "I'm dying of hunger!" he said loudly. "Is there any kosher food here?" The attendees guffawed. He passed in front of the tables laid out with food, twisting his face, and then passed in front of the viewers, staring at the plates they held in their hands. Some of those present, in particular the women, wore expressions of disgust. When a guard approached him, he raised his hands in submission, and backed away quickly. He stood in the middle of the room and informed the audience that he would pray to the good lord to bring him kosher food. Then he leaned down to his coat and took out the phylacteries and prayer shawl. He put the phylacteries on his forehead, and the prayer shawl around his shoulders, pulled a fork out of the coat pocket and started to pray, bowing and shuckling exaggeratedly. Suddenly he stopped, looked at the *tefillin*, sniffed them, licked his lips, and rolled the strips of paper on his fork like spaghetti. He raised the fork to his mouth, and with a strong slurp, he sucked up the paper, chewed it with demonstrable pleasure, and swallowed. The audience laughed loudly. Max took the *tallis* and chewed that up as well, after which he hiccupped loudly, put his head down on the chair, and snored. Applause rose from the audience. "Bravo, bravo!" called Kurt and laughed his horrifying laugh.

On his way back to the barracks, Max knew that he had won for now. The two loaves of bread, several apples, and a pile of sweets resting safely in the pockets of his coat, silently agreed with him. What he didn't know was that this kind of show would become part of his daily routine for the coming years.

## 7

The atmosphere in the barracks had been extremely tense. His neighbors waited with bated breath to know who would return to them, and which of the two beds would be vacated. Dr. Finkelstein had touched everyone's lives. The way in which he managed the life of the barracks with wisdom and patience - in close cooperation with the Germans but without going too far, the fact that, as a doctor, he knew who needed an extra portion of food and who could go without, the natural leadership he demonstrated and the rules that he instituted within the barracks, maintained a relative normalcy. The thought that he would lose his life for nothing, just like that, was hard to digest. Even the following sentence was said aloud, "Maybe we should eliminate Fischer before he eliminates all of us." With the opening of the door, and the entry of both men, the tension vanished instantly.

"Max Fischer accomplished the unbelievable," said Dr. Finkelstein. "He may not be a comic, but he succeeded in making the camp commander's guests laugh until they cried. He also promised to present a show just for us, but in the meantime his valiant efforts tonight brought us this." He presented the loot and continued, "The apples will go to those who I have identified with signs of scurvy. The bread and sweets will be distributed in turn. I ask that whoever can help Max will do so."

## 8

The stinging irony was that Max felt a sense of satisfaction from his forced mission. More than that, with every show, he felt that he was improving his skills as both a clown and an actor. If he could ignore his identity as a prisoner performing under an awful and ongoing threat, he was freer on the stage than ever before. He was not dependent on any text, on a director, or on other actors. In his hands was the flexibility to change the performance in accordance with the reactions of the audience. And yet, he was everything but free. From the moment he understood that he had reached a different planet from the one he had known, and learned what he had to do to keep his friends and himself safe from imminent death, he focused only on how to make the audience laugh.

# 1946, Circus Dantes

"I want you to train your dog to perform in the circus," said Max to Thomas one morning.

Thomas rubbed his eyes in wonder. It was the first time his father had ever asked him for anything. And then he pulled himself together. "What exactly do you want, Papa?"

"Max, I'm Max to you. I want to appear with a dog."

"How much time do I have?" he asked.

"Take the whole day," answered Max and, before Thomas had a chance to react, he added with a smile, "As much time you need."

Thomas hesitated a moment. "I got no idea how to teach you to speak to him."

"I 'don't have any idea,' not 'got no idea,' Thomas. Just because you live in a circus doesn't mean you need to speak like the stagehands here." Thomas smiled to himself. His small provocation worked. He often reached out to his father, seeking Max's closeness, but it only pushed him away. What else could he do?

"And more to the point, let's get started."

Thomas whistled to his yellow dog, Cheetah, who entered the wagon wagging his tail. He looked into the dog's eyes and pointed to Max. "What do you want him to do?" asked Thomas.

"I want him to roll onto his back and then stand up again," Max answered.

"Choose a sign you want to use for this exercise."

Max chose a rolling motion of his finger and Thomas 'translated' it for Cheetah. It didn't even take a full hour and, every time Max rolled his finger, Cheetah rolled onto his back and then stood back up on his feet.

Max, Thomas, and Cheetah started working on the performance of the lead clown.

# 1942, Kaufering Camp, Bavaria

## 1

An invitation to visit Kurt Decker's camp became *le bon ton* among the SS officers and the women in their company. Rumors about the Jewish clown took off. Kurt's assistants hinted to the invitees that there was a shortage of high-quality food in the camp and, thus, the guests brought expensive treats, including cigars and champagne, some of which was indeed distributed to the guests, but most of which were sold on the black market. Kurt knew he had succeeded big-time. This knowledge clarified for him, maybe to his sadness, that his clown had become a goose laying golden eggs, and that it was his job to keep his goose alive, healthy, and satisfied.

Max was allowed to rest during the day and received left over food from the performances which nourished his barracks well. Dr. Finkelstein knew how to take advantage of Max's status to get a hold of critical medicines for residents of the barracks and prisoners at the camp. Max performed at Kurt's orders before the camp's senior staff and the guards and was even liked by them, and so they turned a blind eye to the food he buried in the pockets of his coat.

As Dr. Finkelstein had promised, at night Max performed satirical shows for his friends in the barracks in which he played the Germans as gluttons and drunkards, fools who laughed at every bit of nonsense he performed or, in other words, as subhuman. Thus, the prisoners were granted a short respite, a reprieve from the hell in which they were trapped.

## 2

In contrast to a changing audience in a big city or a show travelling between cities, Max's potential audience was limited: officers, senior members of the party and friends who had heard about him and asked for an invitation to his show. Kurt, even if he had wanted to, didn't dare to sell invitations to a civilian audience. Even in a dictatorship, there are limits to the power of those who aren't at the very top of the pyramid. Therefore, Max was forced to invent more and more shows. He consulted with his friends in the barracks and asked Kurt for permission to host clowns from other barracks. Kurt didn't even try to hide his satisfaction.

"Instead of one clown you want there to be a whole circus, huh? Go ahead, bring friends and musicians, I have plenty of instruments. Just remember that if my friends don't laugh – your friends die." He concluded the conversation with his mad laugh.

Which is how, for example, the love serenade accompanied by the violin was born. The serenade was written for him by Samson Greinrich, his bunkmate and a once respected poet. It was set to music by a well-known veteran violinist by the name of Arnold Katz, who was very happy to return to his vocation and accompany Max's singing before Kurt's guests.

So many of your friends came seeking me
They sought my bed, my love, my company
Sought my warmth each night and day
Each and every one, I pushed away.
Until you appeared, my one true love
Your beauty, your grace, a gift from above
From the very first moment that I saw you,
You stole my heart, how I adore you.
You're the only one I want beside me
In my bed to warm and guide me
To part each morn, is bittersweet
I long for night when again we meet.

They both came to the show – Max and Arnold. Max began by warming up the audience with a few jokes about Jews, and then called loudly, "We have a surprise today!" Arnold entered the room with a serious expression and the violin in hand, bowed deeply and began to play a romantic melody. The audience stared at them in surprise. This was not the performance they had expected. After several moments, Max began to sing. An uncomfortable silence settled over the small audience. Max dared to continue to the second stanza. When he reached the third stanza, there was the sound of a sharp cough. Max knew it was Kurt warning him to hurry up and make everyone laugh. So, when he finished the second sentence of the stanza, "In my bed to warm and guide me" – he pulled a giant, dead rat out of his pocket. He held it by its tail, raised it to his eyes, and continued to sing, "… To part each morn, is bittersweet," and then he held it to his chest and continued, "I long for night when again we met."

Upon seeing the rat, the audience got the punchline and exploded with laughter. With royal grace, Max began to waltz to the sounds of the violin. The audience laughed until they cried, and the sound of Kurt's laugh rose above them all. Suddenly, the violinist stopped and roared, "Gretchen, it's you!" and chased after Max, waving his violin overhead. The show reached its climax when the violinist – in an improvisation that surprised even Max – smashed his violin over Max's head, grabbed the rat from his hands, and ran away. Max was left in the auditorium alone. He shrugged, and said, "No big deal, there are others in the barracks," winked at the audience and followed his friend out.

The next day, Kurt called Max to his office. "There were very senior members of the party in the audience, they loved what you did. Keep performing this bit until I instruct you to stop, is that clear?"

Once again, Max became a star, this time on Kurt Decker's absurdist stage.

# 1942, "The Red Lantern," Munich

## 1

That same night, and the next day, and the day after that, Franz returned to the Red Lantern.

He and Iron listened to the singing of the songstress, but Franz refused Iron's advice to invite her to their table. He knew who she was, and she already knew who he was. A moment before she took the stage the cabaret owner said to her, "The man at the center table in front of the stage who sits with his bodyguard is back again today. Do not go to his table if he doesn't invite you, and if you do go, don't tempt him to drink. He is the commander of the Gestapo in Bavaria; nobody messes around with the likes of him.

Alexandra was frightened. She signaled to the owner of the cabaret to wait a moment with his announcement introducing her to the stage and she checked that Thomas, whom she brought with her to the club on nights she couldn't find a babysitter, was asleep. Her friend Matilda, one of the club dancers, watched him. She looked at him for a long moment and took a deep breath. He is on to me, she thought. He's here because he knows about my connection to Max, he knows about the baron… He knows who Thomas' father is and he's toying with me. Why else would he sit here for three consecutive nights? For a moment, she considered grabbing her son and fleeing to another city to hide. But as the drums began to thunder, she decided to, instead, grab the bull by the horns.

"Please welcome the Baroness!" A single drum played quickly in a steady rhythm, growing louder. The second drum joined in, and then the third. Alexandra came out on stage and stood right in the center of it, like a Greek goddess. She lifted her arms above her head, leveled her gaze straight ahead and right into Franz's eyes, and then lowered her arms in a sharp motion. The thunder of the drums stopped in an instant. Silence fell over the club. In the softest, most sensual voice she could muster, she whispered into the microphone, "Good evening, ladies and gentlemen!" And then she turned toward the light operator and said, "Joachim, turn up the lights a little, so I can see who's here tonight. Thank you." She turned back to the audience, "And again, good evening and welcome to the Lantern. It's me you came to hear, right?"

The audience responded with cheers and applause. "I promise you a show you won't forget. I'm in kind of a... playful mood, to-night. Joachim, shine the spotlight at the table I point to." The bright beam travelled slowly between the tables, accompanied by a quiet, steady beat of the drums until Alexandra pointed at a table far from the stage. "Look, look, an officer from the Luftwaffe. What are you doing here? I thought there was a war going on."

"Yes, but I got leave after I took down six enemy aircraft," the officer called from his seat.

"How many did you shoot down?"

The officer raised six fingers in the air.

"Six airplanes? What a hero!! Can we get some applause, please?" And as the crowd applauded, Alexandra strode to the back of the room and gave him three kisses on each cheek while the audience counted the kisses aloud.

She jumped back on stage and directed the light operator to the table where Franz and Iron sat. "Hello to you, too. You must love me very much; this is your third consecutive night here. Stand up, big guy, so we can see all of you."

Iron stood up with a big smile.

"Wow! You really are big, a giant! And who is that with you, your bodyguard?"

The tuba reacted with a low snort, and the audience laughed.

"I'm his," said Iron, and Franz avoided Alexandra's gaze.

"Today you're my gallant knight, okay? I'm announcing a boxing match here on stage after my show and I'm putting a hundred marks on my knight, this big guy." She started to sensually remove her black glove, finger by finger. When she was done, she threw it into the audience. "Gloves are off, who's ready to take on my knight? No one? Apparently, you truly are frightening, big boy." And again, the tuba reacted with a low note.

Alexandra signaled the orchestra to begin with a wild drinking song accompanied by the raucous horns. She sang, boy did she sing, and danced like she was floating between the orchestra, the stage, and the audience. And when the orchestra was particularly loud, she came down into the audience. She pinched this one's cheek, patted that one on the shoulder, and also whispered in Franz's ear, "Stay after the show tonight, my dear."

At the end of her performance, Alexandra parted from the audience with a light-hearted song, and hurried to her dressing room, where little Thomas slept soundly under Matilda's watchful eye. "Can you watch him for another few hours?" she asked. The young Matilda, as always, was happy to help. Alexandra was the one who had recognized her talent when she danced on the streets of Munich hoping someone would toss her a few coins. Alexandra recommended her to the manager of the Lantern, who gave her a job, and they became dear friends. Alexandra thanked her, peeled herself out of the tight dress, and chose a more modest one. She put on perfume, touched up her make-up, threw a last look at the sleeping boy, and headed out. Just before she disappeared from sight, she stopped. "Matilda, if something happens tonight, and I don't come back here, promise me you'll take care of my son."

"Of course, but why would you say such a thing?"

"I don't know, just feeling frightened tonight…"

"Nonsense, no one would dare touch you, you know that."

Alexandra wrapped herself up in the character of a confident woman, a member of the elite, and went out to the audience who were now watching an acrobatics performance. She circulated with a beaming smile, stopped to speak with this one, to kiss that one on the cheek, and to sip a beer with another.

She dilly-dallied, taking her time, so the Gestapo officer would not realize she was eager to speak with him, to understand why he came to her shows and find out what he knows about her. In a strange way, she was drawn to the danger like a moth to a flame. Did she want to end the game? To shorten the agony of foot- dragging? She was afraid her haste would betray her anxiety and confirm his suspicions. She made sure he was always in her line of sight, and she realized that the giant was no longer sitting next to him. When she couldn't stand the tension any longer, she approached him with an easy, confident gait for someone who already knew he was the state's Gestapo commander. She smiled a wide smile and said, "I see a seat has opened up here. May I?"

"Or course, of course," answered Franz, getting to his feet. He pulled the chair out for her. She saw that he blushed, truly blushed.

"You compliment me greatly, sir, with your visits to the club.

Allow me to order you a drink, my treat, and don't say, no!" Franz deferred but Alexandra waved to the waiter, "Freddy, two piccolos on my tab, please. Yes, on my tab." She looked back at Franz. "So, with whom do I have the pleasure…?"

"My name is Franz Schmidt, and I have been a fan of yours for years."

"Years? I don't remember you being her before…"

"No, not from here. You sing very nicely, but I am not here for the singing."

"No? Then why?"

"Heaven truly knows that thou art false as hell," Franz called in a thunderous voice. Without hesitation or reason, Alexandra responded as she had every time Othello roared his harsh words at her, there on the stage of the Berlin theater, "To whom, my lord? With whom? How…" And then she fell silent in horror, when she realized how easily she had given herself away.

"Alexandra Brecholdt, the great actress, sits with me in a nightclub and plays Desdemona. I must be dreaming."

Alexandra pulled herself together and answered calmly, "That's right, it's me, but now I am a singer."

"You must have a good reason to do what you are doing."

"Yes, with my divorce from the baron, I was left with a baby, and I'm embarrassed to show my face in Berlin. Is that a good enough reason?"

"I have admired you from the day I first saw you on stage. I spent half my wages buying tickets to your plays. At night, I dreamt that it was me standing across from you on stage saying the immortal lines, and to me you answered, like you did just this minute without knowing you were fulfilling the most secret wish of one of your greatest fans."

Alexandra got confused, but her face remained stalwart. I will not let him catch me, definitely not in this kind of honey trap, she said to herself. "Do you have a pen?" she asked. She picked up the fountain pen he held out to her, and as she had done thousands of times in Berlin, she signed on the bottom of the cup with a curling hand, "To my dearest Franz, Alexandra Brecholdt." To her surprise, he thanked her excitedly.

At that moment, Freddy arrived not with the two cheap bottles of piccolo she had ordered, but with a bottle of Dom Perignon, the fine French champagne. She only hoped that the cost of the bottle would not be deducted from her wages. The ritual of uncorking the bottle and pouring the champagne into the flutes, allowed her to calculate the rest of the duel.

"I must speak with the other guests; can you wait for me until I return?" she asked with the most charming smile she was able to muster.

"Of course I will wait, it's not every day that one gets to meet the Mrs. Brecholdt," answered Franz and clinked his glass with hers.

Alexandra circulated among the tables for a full hour. One ordered her a glass of something for which he would pay a hefty price without knowing that she was drinking soda water, another asked for her signature, and a third, a tall colonel in a combat uniform, flirted with her boorishly.

"What connection do you have with this uncultured riffraff?" asked Franz when she returned to his table.

"I have a child to support."

"And do you enjoy it?"

"That's not a fair question, but I will answer. Of course, I enjoy it. I sing, I dance, and act for anyone who comes to see me to forget their troubles. Every night is a new challenge, and at its end, I mostly feel satisfaction, like at the end of a successful play. And what about you, without knowing what you do – do you always enjoy your work? Or the talented musicians in the orchestra, do they always enjoy playing here in the cabaret and not in a concert hall?" Alexandra drank the champagne Franz poured for her, her face displaying an easy calm she didn't feel. She wondered what was going through his mind. While she hid her fears, Franz tried to decide how to answer her, the one and only Alexandra Brecholdt, the woman he had admired for so many years. And while he was searching for words, she finished drinking from the crystal glass in her hand, put it down on the table and threw him a beaming smile. "It's time to go home, thank you for hosting me at your table."

"May I escort you home?" Franz erupted hastily.

## 2

Alexandra decided not to take Thomas with her in the Gestapo car. She wasn't sure if it would indeed take her home or to some well-known Gestapo basement that would be her end. As a Jewish child, according to the Nuremberg laws, it was best he sleep at Matilda's. She placed several bills in Matilda's hand for her troubles and asked her to watch him carefully until she came. Alexandra knew she could count on her.

She returned to the auditorium and found Franz sitting at his table, his hand cradling a half-filled glass of champagne. When he saw her, he jumped out of his seat. And then bowed deeply and cleared the way for her to walk before him. As they exited, while Franz looked around for the black Mercedes, the same drunken colonel who had flirted with Alexandra in the club approached them. "You're going out with this mouse, instead of with me?" he cried. "Absolutely not, you're coming with me…"

Franz strode forward to block his way and was shoved aside by the officer, who took another step and grabbed Alexandra's shoulder. There was an immediate, howl of pain and the officer collapsed to the ground.

"Are you okay, Commander?" asked Iron.

"Yes, please check how the singer is."

It had taken Franz many months to teach Iron not to break necks.

"I'm sorry I didn't stand at the entrance, but sat in the car, it won't happen again."

"Has anything like this happened to you before, Mrs. Brecholdt?" asked Franz with worry.

"No, not like this, in general I get along with them."

"The combat officers return for short leaves before they go back to the eastern front. They are desperate for a woman and a little warmth… It will happen now, more and more…"

"What should I do with him, Commander?" asked Iron.

"it seems water on him to wake him and leave him be."

In the car, Franz asked Alexandra if she wanted to have a glass of cognac with him and calm her nerves. She knew Thomas was in good hands, and her intuition was that Franz did not intend to harm her. But mostly, she needed the drink and, more than that, she needed the conversation to clarify what his intentions were towards her.

They entered a dark bar and sat in the corner. Franz's bodyguard sat not far from them. The waiter brought a bottle of cognac and two glasses to their table. After the second shot, Franz's tongue loosened. He told her about himself, about his childhood, about the father he never had. "I will tell you something personal, that no one knows about me," he said and poured himself a third glass which he downed in a single shot. He hesitated a moment and then told her about the Jew who rescued him and his mother from the rubbish heap and made sure to provide them with a home and pay for his education.

Alexandra wondered if he was making up details of his past in order to milk a similar confession from her, but she couldn't ignore the honesty that was apparent in his words and in his eyes that testified to his speaking the truth. "Where are they now?" she asked politely.

"They fled to America before the Führer came to power," said Franz. Alexandra realized she was sitting with Franz Schmidt, one of the most dangerous men in Bavaria and, she, Alexandra, was again the actress who conquered Berlin's theatrical stage, and they were conversing pleasantly. She was infused with a sense of calm.

"I've always wanted to know, the Desdemona you brought to life on the day that God himself placed me in the theater to see you in your debut performance on the stage – was it your own interpretation?"

Alexandra smiled. "When I was given the opportunity to play Desdemona, I imagined my mother."

"Your mother?" asked Franz. Alexandra told him about her mother's heroic behavior and fell silent.

Franz was also quiet, but the sudden spark in his eye said more than words. That same night, Iron returned Alexandra safely to Matilda's house. He waited for her there until she came out with Thomas in her arms. The warm space inside the Mercedes also warmed her heart. When she went up to bed, she went over the strange evening in her mind and, to her surprise, she realized that she wanted to see Franz again.

## 3

After less than twenty-four hours, just before she got on stage, the owner of the cabaret approached her excitedly. "It seems he likes you; he's sitting in his usual spot. Alone, without the gorilla."

"Don't call him a gorilla," said Alexandra with a sharpness that surprised even her. At the end of the show, with the departure of most of the guests, she went to Franz's table and he immediately stood respectfully.

"I'm sorry, they pay me my wages." She smiled and sat.

Franz signaled the waiter, who brought them drinks. "I know, you need to do your work. I'm sorry to disturb you, but I was enchanted by our conversation last night and I wanted to continue it."

"It was a special evening for me too, but I cannot send my son home with a babysitter every night and stay out until the wee hours."

"Then why don't we meet comfortably for coffee some afternoon?"

During the next three months, Alexandra and Franz met once a week in the afternoon. They talked, laughed, enacted the protagonists of plays, sometimes he was the hero and she the heroine, and sometimes she demonstrated her interpretation of a particular scene. Alexandra loved their meetings and, on the occasions when their weekly meeting was cancelled, she found herself disappointed.

## 4

On their way to the office, Franz asked Iron to join him for breakfast.

Iron watched Franz squirm in his seat. "Hmm, you know, sometimes you help me with investigations, identify if the person before me is lying or not, if he has hate in his heart or not." Iron nodded.

"Can you tell me what Alexandra thinks for me? It's very important to me."

Iron thought for a long time before answering. "What do you mean by the word, 'thinks?'"

"Does she... does she love me?"

Iron shrugged and chose his words carefully. "She enjoys your company, Commander. She also appreciates you very much and trusts you. I think..."

"Be straightforward, Iron."

"I think that she is not drawn to you like a female in heat is drawn to a male." Amazement and anger mingled in the look Franz threw at Iron. "I'm sorry, Commander, you asked me to be straightforward – and that is as straightforward as I could say it. In animals, it is easy to recognize attraction between a male and a female. You don't see in their eyes what humans mean by love. In the animals within us, humans, it's easy to identify the initial things. But the human concept of 'love' I don't understand, and I don't know how to identify. I'm sorry if that's not the answer you were expecting."

The wildfire that had burned in Franz's eyes for a moment, went out with his embarrassment in front of Iron. "Thank you, you helped me a great deal," he said and sank into thought. Iron wondered if he was right not to mention the other man, whom Alexandra's soul was tied to.

"What's going on with the commander? What do you mean he invited you to breakfast all of a sudden?" asked Suzanna when he walked out of Franz's office, but she didn't wait for an answer. "Since you took him to the Red Lantern, he has become a different person. He's happy, he smiles, and for three months now, he's been going out the same day every week for an 'afternoon meeting' I know nothing about. When, exactly, do you plan on telling me?"

Iron looked at her with embarrassment. "He met a woman at the Lantern," he said.

"I knew it!" cried Suzanna. "Now do tell, why did you stop, who is it?"

"A woman by the name of Alexandra Brecholdt," answered Iron.

Suzanna choked. She looked at Iron with amazement. "The actress? Are you joking? She's here in Munich, singing in a cabaret? Are you sure it's Alexandra Brecholdt? What?"

Iron held back his laughter. He had never seen Suzanna so worked up before. "I'll continue, if you'll just let me," he smiled. "Yes, it's the actress. She's a cabaret singer, she calls herself..."

"The Baroness!" Suzanna again interrupted him. "The Baroness is Mrs. Brecholdt? The commander was a fan of hers back when he . was a policeman in Berlin. I cannot imagine how much money he wasted on the plays she was in. It's no wonder that he's so happy. So, what's going on between them?"

Iron hesitated a moment. "He loves her, I think." Iron continued and told her about their last conversation. "I think I scared him. He wanted to get closer to her..."

"I'll talk to him," said Suzanna with determination and knocked on the door of Franz's office. A full hour later, she walked out of his office with a victorious smile. "The commander wants to go out immediately," she said to Iron and added nothing more.

## 5

Franz lingered another few minutes, made a single phone call, and then asked Iron to join him. With a confident step he entered the café where Alexandra awaited him. Iron waited in the car.

"I so enjoy your friendship, I love your personality," he said to her as soon as he sat down. "Your intelligence and your laugh. I can give you the security that you are lacking when you are alone. It's true Iron takes you home every night from the Red Lantern and no one bothers you, but it must be clear to you that backstage at a cabaret is no decent place for a small child... I live in a huge apartment, alone... You will have your own room there, and Thomas will have his own room. You will have help with Thomas around the clock..." Franz was silent. He didn't dare look her in the eye.

Alexandra drank quickly from the glass of wine she was holding. "Franzie, my sweet, you are charming, smart, cultured... you are everything that is lacking in Munich and that I was missing – even with my husband. But... but..."

"You're not attracted to me... Shhh, don't answer, I know that I'm not the material that is attractive to women, but I'm willing to forego..." He dropped his eyes. "I will not force myself on you, I will not keep you from meeting other men, if you wish. Just please, not in public, and not at my place... Not with us at home."

Alexandra looked at him and kept herself from bursting into laughter. One of the strongest and most frightening men in Germany was like a besotted schoolboy caught peeking in the window of his neighbor. She knew she had nothing to lose. He would be a perfect partner for her, and aside from how cultured he was, he would provide security for her and for Thomas. Who would dare harass the Gestapo Commander's woman? And of course, there was also the matter of financial security. She calculated that if she took Franz up on his offer, each month, a healthy sum would remain in her hands that she would be able to send to her mother in Berlin.

It was as if Franz read her mind. "Alexandra my dear, think of how much you will save each month. You will have quite a bit of money to send to your parents." She glared at him sharply. "I'm sorry, but my profession dictates that I gather all the information necessary to protect your parents and us."

Alexandra wondered what else he knew about her, but in fact, the simple and straight forward apology by a person as powerful as he, and the way he shrugged his shoulders, was what convinced her – more than anything else that had been said up to that point – to acquiesce.

About a week later, Alexandra and Thomas recreated their home in the Gestapo commander's official residence. He knew who Thomas' father was, it didn't take much to see the likeness between him and Max Fischer, but he kept the knowledge that it was he who had led to Max's imprisonment to himself.

## 6

Alexandra's life improved beyond recognition. The financial struggle was behind her, no-one harassed her at work, the housekeeper released her from the work of cleaning and cooking, and a nanny took care of Thomas, who grew up to be a smart, attentive, and curious boy. Franz made sure he was educated at the best institutions in the city and also paid for private teachers in particular subjects. When he was six years old, Thomas already knew how to speak German, French, and English, he had begun to learn to read, and even studied music.

Franz turned out to be a perfect partner. They conducted ongoing conversations where they weren't aware of just how much time had passed . Franz was not afraid to bring home books that were illegal to publish and distribute in the Third Reich. "I can always say that I read them to learn the ways of the enemies among us," he said with a wink. Which is how, for example, Alexandra got to again enjoy the work of Erich Maria Remarque, whose books of criticism about the Great War taught her about her father's misery.

With gentle pressure from Franz, Alexandra cut back her performances at the Red Lantern to three nights a week. Franz also made sure she travelled to Berlin with Thomas to see her parents. Alexandra was pleased to discover that the dedicated care her mother gave to her father had improved his condition.

At night, before she fell asleep in the living room of her parents' home with Thomas next to her, her mother said, "It's a good thing you didn't take my advice and insisted on having Thomas. My grandson will grow up to be a man with his head on straight. He is sharp and sensitive. I hope his life will be better than ours."

Alexandra asked them to move to Munich. "That way we can be closer, and you can see Thomas..." she said.

"We cannot leave our home, and the printing house," her mother answered. "Your father would not be able to withstand that kind of change..."

Alexandra said goodbye to her parents. She knew that from now on, she could take care of all their needs. One could say, she was now completely satisfied, although Germany's growing hardship in the war stood in sharp contrast to her comfortable life.

# 1944, Munich

"What's bothering you, Franzie?" asked Alexandra. They both sat opposite the burning fireplace with glasses of port in hand. Alexandra felt the discomfort that enveloped him.

"Work is bothering me, but I can't elaborate. I can only say that Germany is being squeezed from every front and I'm responsible for fighting a growing number of opponents against the government and the Führer. It's not easy…"

"That's nothing new, Franzie. But something else is bothering you today…"

"Damn!" exclaimed Franz, "You and Iron read me like an open book!"

"Don't change the subject, tell me."

"I'm sorry, but I really don't know how to tell you. I heard terrible news from Berlin. A bomb was dropped from a plane - it was a direct hit on your parents' printing house. There were no survivors."

"The printing house was destroyed?" asked Alexandra.

"Alexandra, my sweet, your parents… they were there."

Alexandra fell onto his chest in tears. That whole night she sat and told him stories about her parents. About the joy and love she experienced in her childhood. About the passion for books and theater she cultivated from her father, and the talent for music she inherited from her mother. She told him at length about her father's illness, and about her mother's courage. Franz drank in her words thirstily. For one night, the personal grief of the woman he loved erased all the nightmares of the war.

"How did Alexandra take the difficult news?" Iron asked Franz while driving him to work the following morning.

"It's hard for her," answered Franz. "We need your help," he added.

"Anything you say, Commander," answered Iron.

"Go back to my place, take Thomas to school and, after school, pick him up and take him home to your place, tell him we went on vacation."

"For how long, Commander?"

"Until I let you know to bring him back to us. Alexandra needs some time. She needs to say goodbye to her parents."

When Alexandra woke from sleeping, she hurried to call Franz. "Where is Thomas?" she asked.

"With Iron," answered Franz.

"Okay. As long as he doesn't tell him anything. I want to tell him."

Over the coming days, Alexandra cried for her parents. She barely got out of bed, she refused to eat and barely spoke, not even to Franz. After three days, Franz went into her room with a steaming cup of coffee and a fragrant piece of cake.

"You must get better, my dear," he said. "You must be strong. If not for yourself or for me, then for your son. Thomas is having a great time with Iron, as was expected, but he needs you."

"I always knew that one day I would depart from them," said Alexandra. "But not this way, not like this…" Franz gently stood her on her feet and hugged her firmly.

That same day, Alexandra arrived at school to fetch Thomas as she always did - wearing make-up and a big smile. They had lunch and she told him that his grandfather and grandmother had alighted to heaven. Thomas asked if they would bring him back stars as a present, and a gloomy smile settled on Alexandra's face.

# 1948-1949, Berlin, Circus Dantes

## 1

Max looked in the mirror, once again, seeing-not-seeing the eyes that stared back at him. The merry cheers of the audience, the thunder of the drums, the blare of the trumpets, and the low oompah of the tubas - none of it penetrated the wall insulating his senses.

At that moment, his whole world was focused on the one repetitive action he executed once, sometimes twice a day, day after day, week after week, year after year. Max pulled a bald wig encircled with a snarl of pink cotton over his head. He carefully spread a thick layer of white paint on his face. With a thin brush, he painted two high, semi-circles black as coal, for eyebrows, added black liner around his eyes, a large mouth, wide and smiling, and a big beauty mark on his right cheek. Max began to paint his eyelids a glittering blue. Last but not least, it was time for the red, a color a clown clearly cannot do without. He painted wide, red lines around his lips, drawing them far from the edges of his mouth.

In precise concert with the moment, he put down the red brush, the excited call of the ring master could be heard in the background, "Please welcome the funniest clown on earth, the man who has made more children laugh than anyone else in history. No one knows from where he came or to where he is going... Here's - Anonymous!"

Max covered his nose with a red, rubber ball, stood up, and strode towards the circus ring. The roar of the crowd, the cheers of the children, and the sounds of the noisy circus orchestra reached his ears. Through it all, in the background, from some undefined direction, he heard the sound that accompanied him day and night, through wakefulness and dreams, the sound that never let up: the peeling wails of the crazy laugh.

From the moment Anonymous burst into the rollicking circus ring, nothing was left of Max, even the crazy laugh was nearly silenced. Were it not for the dead eyes that ceaselessly scanned the crowd as if searching for something lost, almost nothing would connect Max to Anonymous the Clown, who elicited howls of laughter and tears of joy with the skill of an artist.

As soon as Anonymous entered the ring, Cheetah galloped forward, barking loudly. "Help!" yelled the clown, pulling a bone out of his huge clown pants and throwing it towards the angry dog who ran after the bone. Anonymous turned to the audience and cried, "Who's scared of a little dog?"

"You are! You are!" the children yelled back. They became like putty in his hands.

Anonymous continued his absurd shenanigans with Cheetah. One moment he pulled on the dog's tail, and the next he ran from the dog who caught hold of his pants and left him standing in nothing but red polka-dotted boxers. Another moment, he chased after the dog, riding a unicycle, and the next the dog chased him, hitting the wheel of his vehicle and sending Anonymous flying into the air. He landed, rolled, and popped up, a giant balloon stuck to his nose. For dessert, Anonymous lifted a small child of about five years old from the audience and sat him on Cheetah's back and the dog took the child for a ride around the ring – the clown skipping alongside, cheerful and good-hearted. All of the clown's attention was apparently focused on the child, but still, his eyes continued to scan the crowd in search of something.

When Anonymous left the ring, he disappeared from the world. With every step that carried him away from the noise inside the tent, the clown dissipated and Max, the man, returned. The sound of the mad laugh returned, destroying his serenity. He never returned for a bow, because he retreated from that world and would not reappear until the next performance.

Max sat before the mirror and stared at the tired character reflected back at him. His hands reached for the tin clown with the drum and wound the key in its back. The toy clown began to bang on the drum hanging at his hip, with his right hand, and then his left. Max took a sponge from the bowl sitting in front of him and began to remove the make-up from his face. The moment he finished, the wind-up toy finished drumming. "To be or not to be," he whispered to the figure reflected in the mirror, and the figure did not reply...

## 2

"How was it?" asked Alexandra before she got on stage. Max had removed all his make-up and had just entered their wagon.

"Wonderful. The audience was mine from the first moment. Even Cheetah improves from show to show. I think he enjoys the role. I have to cool off," he added. "I'm going out to walk around town a little, I need a drink."

"It's Thomas' birthday," said Alexandra. "Don't you want to be a part of it?"

"I said I need a break, what wasn't clear?" he answered.

Max looked in the mirror, powdered his face to look pale and, with a skilled hand, he added wrinkles, stuck on a thick moustache, and put on heavy-framed glasses. It was hard to recognize him, quite impossible for anyone who hadn't seen him for a long time.

He entered a smoky bar in the heart of Berlin, whose address he got from the trapeze artists. "A bar of your standards," they said, "For upper class folks." He sat down at one of the big tables, ordered a dark beer from the heavy-set waitress and studied the crowd.

The easiest to identify were the Americans. They spoke loudly and treated everyone else, in particular the Germans, like they were in charge. Ironically, it was the Germans Max had a hard time under-standing. They were different from the elite that Max knew when he lived in the city, and also from the riffraff who populated the beer gardens of Munich. They were the generation produced by the war, educated in Nazi youth movements, who had experienced the hor-rors of war and the destruction of the Third Reich. As hard as he tried to have a conversation with one of them, he could not find a common language. In the meantime, the waitress arrived, put a paper coaster on the table, a glass of beer on it and marked a single line on the coaster. Max drank his beer quickly and asked for another. The waitress brought it and marked another line. Three lines had already accumulated on the round coaster when Max realized nothing would come of his hanging around and signaled to the waitress for the bill.

Just then, two young men sat down next to him, carrying on a lively conversation. Max, who had already stood up, sat back down and signaled the waitress that he had changed his mind and wanted another glass. The young men spoke Hebrew, a language he had learned from his father in his youth but had not heard or spoken since the night of the last Passover *seder* his mother held in her home, in another world. Max listened to their words and his heart pounded. It wasn't just the language itself that attracted him, but the content of their words. They spoke about Nazi leaders and officers who had fled justice and went into hiding around the world. The names Adolf Eichmann and Dr. Mengele came up over and over. "I'm sure that they're hiding out either in Brazil or Argentina," one of them said. "No," answered his friend, "Argentina or Chile."

Max had heard enough. He got up from his seat, paid his bill, put on his hat, and left. He then went about his usual routine. He bought a newspaper and dug into the notices on the back page, where they reported about war criminals that one country or another had succeeded in capturing.

## 3

The circus was sleeping. Max silently entered his wagon and was not surprised to find Alexandra awake. Every time he went out at night, she waited for him to return.

"What exactly are you looking for at these bars when you go out?" she asked. Max looked at her and didn't answer. "It's a shame you weren't part of Thomas' birthday party. Everyone from the circus celebrated with him, except you."

"I'm sorry. I told you before, I cannot be a father, I don't want to deceive him... They would have asked me to make a toast with some birthday wishes for him. What could I have wished him? A better life than mine?"

"I'm not the one who needs to understand. Thomas is. You explain it to him, I..."

"Hold me, hold me, and chase this crazy laugh from my ears, give me back my life, my sanity..."

Alexandra slipped closer to him, kissed him, and dragged him to bed. She knew this was the only way to drive away the demons and the crazy laughter, even if only for a few precious moments.

**4**

Thomas didn't fall asleep that night. His father's absence from his twelfth birthday party reopened the wound in his heart. At dawn they met on the steps of Max's wagon. Thomas' sad face was testament to his mood, "Why do you hate me?" he asked. "Why do you direct all the anger and sorrow you feel for your murdered family, at me?" Do you hate me because I'm a German? It was you that chose a German woman, why is it my fault? Why don't you want me?"

Max was amazed by the power and directness of his questions. "I don't hate you, Thomas. If only I had the emotional strength to be your father. It is not your fault, child. You are wonderful, your mother is proud of you, and rightly so." Max took a deep breath. "But I am a Jew, and spilling Jewish blood is permitted. This is our story, the story of a cursed people of which I am a part. It is my history, but not yours. Stick to your mother, you will be safe with her... With me, you have no protection, no future."

"Papa, the Nazis aren't here anymore, evil was defeated, they won't let them do it again..."

Max responded with a bitter laugh. "You think only the Germans hate us? You are so wrong. Everyone hates us. You think Churchill, Roosevelt, and Stalin didn't know why the Jews were being transferred from across the whole of Europe to Poland? You think they didn't know where the trains were taking them? Why didn't they do anything to stop the extermination machine? Why didn't they bomb the train tracks that led my people to the death camps? Why? Why?" Max continued quietly, at almost a whisper. "Because they didn't care if another million Jews died, because like the Germans, they hate us. And you willingly choose me, a Jew, to be your father?"

"I'm not choosing you, and you didn't choose me. You are my father, and whether you like it or not, I am your son. Don't worry about me. If I meet the murderers who killed my brother, my grandfather and grandmother, I'll send my big cats after them… They won't kill me, and I won't let them hurt you either!"

Max hugged his son who had matured before his very eyes, and a fire began to burn in them, where they had been deadened for so long. "Thomas, I look at you, and I see myself as a boy. Everything I learned, I absorbed like quicksand. Like you, I was afraid of nothing. When I was young, everyone wanted to be my friend, I was king of my forest, and look at what happened to me. They took everything from me. My profession, my honor, my property, my family. And I had promised my family I would keep them safe, just like you're promising me, that nothing would happen to them. I promised, and couldn't keep that promise."

He looked at Thomas more tenderly than ever before and asked quietly, "Do you know why I'm a clown?" Thomas shook his head, no. "Because he wanted to humiliate me – it amused him." Max's quiet voice became a yell when he repeated the last line, "It amused him!" and then he whispered again, "It amused him, Thomas, and if I didn't make him laugh, then he shot one of my brothers… I don't want anyone to die again because of me, that's why I'm a clown." Max nodded his head up and down and again his voice became a yell, "I will be ready, and they will not murder anyone because I'm not funny, you hear? No one else will be murdered because of me!" His voice cracked, and he fought unsuccessfully to hold back his tears,

"I can't be a father, I must not be a father, don't you understand?"

Thomas tried to hug him, but Max recoiled His eyes that had just flashed and cried, deadened once again.

Thomas' face did not reveal what had seeped into his innocent heart. He held back the tears in his own eyes, he would not cry now, not in front of his father.

He whistled to his dog and entered the empty tent and, there, in front of his loyal pet, he burst into heartbreaking sobs. "You don't care if I'm a Jew, right?" he whispered, and his dog licked away his tears with unconditional love.

## 5

When Thomas recovered from his crying, he entered Alexandra's wagon and asked her for a copy of the Old Testament. She rummaged through a locked trunk and pulled out the copy of the bible Franz had left with her, a book he had received from his adopted father, the good Avram.

"Take it," she said. "Every person leaves us something, so that we may pass it along."

Thomas looked at her. "Please leave me alone for the next little while. I want to figure out a few things, I want to understand where I came from."

After a week passed, Thomas burst into his mother's room in a whirlwind. "Mama, I'm twelve years old, another year from now, I will be called to the Torah, I'll celebrate my bar mitzvah." Alexandra, surprised, was silent for a long moment, and then she smiled a wide smile.

"I'll go tell Papa," said Thomas.

# 6

Max was left alone in his emotional turmoil. He didn't know what he could do to distance his son from his religion, his nation, and mostly from his god. He remembered his own bar mitzvah, the excitement he felt knowing that, from that moment on, he alone was responsible for his sins before God. Do you even exist? he thought to himself. You, our merciful Father of justice and truth? If so, then how could you have brought this cruelty upon us? What happened? Did you miss the sacrifices offered you on the altar of the Holy Temple in Jerusalem that you yourself destroyed two thousand years ago? Did you decide that sheep and cows were too lowly, so you placed all of European Jewry on the altar? And if you turned Europe into a sanctum, you anointed Hitler as your high priest? Hitler?! Was it you, Lord of War, whom he served when he murdered so many of your children? And you, you who once knew how to take pride in the deaths you sowed with your own hands. After the tenth plague you imposed on Egypt, you said, "I did this, I and not an angel." Have you grown old? Weak? Have you become soulless and so you sent a crazy *goy* to do the work? Your work? You and your slave, Hitler, did not stop at a million, or two million, or even three. Six million Jews were murdered, six million! Are you satisfied with the thorough work of your slave? Will you grant him, Adolf Hitler, a divine iron cross for his excellent service? Will you give it to him personally? Will he be rewarded in heaven?

How is it possible that Jews who witnessed their own children, their fathers and mothers, brothers and sisters, their spouses go up in smoke through the chimneys, how do they recite each day, "How manifold are your creations, Oh Lord! In wisdom you have made them all..." In wisdom??? What I saw was made with ugliness and Satanic ignorance, not divine wisdom!

## 7

For the length of a year, Thomas studied diligently in anticipation of being called to the Torah. When the year passed, the Reform synagogue in the suburbs of Berlin filled with worshippers. Max, who asked not to be called to the Torah for an *aliyah*, looked around with amazement. Everything was both familiar and, at the same time, strange. The playing of the organ on the Sabbath, the prayers in German, the curtain on the ark that opened with the push of a button, the women sitting beside their husbands, their sons and daughters, instead of in a separate area. Reform Judaism was different from the Orthodox Sabbath services he remembered from his childhood. He did not open a prayer book, but from time to time he absent-mindedly joined in with the congregation, humming the melodies he still remembered. He got to his feet when everyone stood, sat when they all sat.

The moment came when it was time to call the bar mitzvah boy. The cantor called, "He shall stand and come forward, Tom, son of Alexandra Brecholdt..." Thomas stood and looked pleadingly at Max, but Max stayed seated. The rabbi signaled to Alexandra to join them, and Max realized that this, too, was the custom among the Reform Jews. He watched the three slowly approach the pulpit. Forgotten images from his childhood rose to his mind. Here he himself stood at the *bima* with his own father, who whispered in his ear, "Show everyone that you are a son of the Fischer family, show them how beautifully you read..."

"*Barchu et Adonai hamevorach...*" The prayer was heard in the original language, and in Thomas' loud, clear voice. "Praise the Lord, the Source of blessing."

"*Baruch adonai mevorach le'olam va'ed,*" answered Max along with the rest of the congregants. Praised be the Lord, Source of blessing, throughout all time." He heard his son sing the ancient Hebrew words in his pure, strong voice, with precision. His soul stirred within him, just as the souls of a million Jewish fathers before him had been stirred, when their sons became a bar mitzvah... With the completion of the blessings, Max stood. He saw the rabbi give Alexandra a printed page, and she started to read from it. Max heard in his head the booming, melodical voice of his own father, echoing in the space of the great synagogue of Berlin and, in a loud voice that shook the walls of the reform synagogue, he repeated his father's words, the words said by a million Jewish fathers before him at their sons' bar mitzvahs: "*Baruch sh'patarani me'onsho shel ze!*" Blessed is He who has released me from responsibility for him!

Most of those in attendance, Alexandra among them, didn't understand why the youth who read from the Torah with such confidence collapsed in his mother's arms and burst into tears. But Thomas knew. He knew the meaning of Max's declaration before a room full of witnesses, that he and no other had been responsible until this moment for Thomas' sins; Max declared that he was Thomas' father.

At age thirteen, Thomas had won the first significant battle of his life – his father recognized him as his son.

He did not know there would be more battles to win.

# 1945, Munich

## 1

Kurt Decker rarely left the Kaufering Camp which he command-ed. At the camp, he was God, he determined who lived and who died. But when he was summoned to SS headquarters "for a special command" in Munich, about a half an hour's drive from the camp, there he was just one of many, a lowly officer. Kurt was amazed by the sight of the mayhem at headquarters. People were running around with no direction from above, doors slamming, yelling from every direction. For the first time since the beginning of the war, it dawned on him that the Third Reich would inevitably fall. He sat in the auditorium with the other commanders summoned from camps across Bavaria.

"Our forces are strong, and we will succeed in overcoming our enemies," said the region commander. "But, it seems, one or two camps may fall to the Americans who are getting closer, and we cannot allow our records to fall into their hands. You must immedi-ately start burning the archives in the camps under your command. Is that clear?"

## 2

In the officer's club, after two or three glasses of schnapps, the knot in Kurt's throat started to loosen. He joked around with the officers around him, as he was wont to do, bragged about his success, and laughed his mad laugh.

The schnapps continued to flow and, very soon, a group of drunken, light-hearted SS officers headed out, making their way to the Red Lantern, whose reputation had travelled far and wide.

## 3

The winds of war raged, but backstage at the Red Lantern cabaret, now co-owned by Franz Schmidt, Alexandra prepared for her show.

She sat down in front of the mirror, stretched her cat-like body, took off her bra, and threaded her long legs into the shiny black corset she used as a dress and pulled it up. The corset pushed her breasts up so that it looked as if her full bosom might escape. Garters and black, silk, fishnet stockings, black stilettos, and a final look in the mirror. She smiled to herself. Every man in the audience would want her, without doubt. They would want her, but they would have to suffice with sharing a drink with her beside their table, and a fluttery kiss on the cheek. In those days, Alex did not have moments as magical as those just before getting on stage.

"Ladies and gentlemen, from Berlin, the capital of the Third Reich, the singer, the actress, and the woman desired by the whole world, please welcome, the Baroness!"

Alexandra slipped her leg out in front of the curtain. She kicked it high, and then lowered it back down again slowly. She leaped out

into the spotlight, her hands waving above her head, her fists opening and closing in time with the loud music. Energy bubbled from
her like a vernal spring and the audience responded with applause
and cheers. She moved across the stage with the sensual lightness of
a tiger, approached the microphone, held it gently and stroked it in
her hands. Even the men who didn't understand why this fluttering
motion drove them out of their minds applauded and cheered.

And then she sang. She opened with a low, erotic, nearly mascu-
line voice. She sang about the loneliness of soldiers at war, about the
loneliness of the women left behind. Every soldier in the hall, even
if he hadn't endangered his life in some heroic battle, identified with
the soothing lyrics, the whispered voice, and the heart crying over
the death of love. The few who were capable of understanding the
anti-war message that lurked between the words were hypnotized
by the longing in her blue eyes and the movement of her lithesome
body. Near the end of the song, Alex signaled the orchestra with
her hand, and it quieted. The lights of the stage went out except for
one spotlight, which lit her face with a thin halo. She screamed the
scream of a woman who receives the news of Job. Her clear voice
echoed through the entire hall, and then again became a broken
whisper, until it faded completely.... The club was silent.

Just for a moment.

The audience rose to its feet and burst into applause and cheers.
Alexandra took a deep bow and signaled for the orchestra to play
a lighthearted drinking song. She came down from the stage and
danced with the guests of the cabaret who gave themselves over
to her like clay in the hands of a sculptor. Not one of the guests
imagined that behind the radiant singer, hid the mother of a child,
fathered by a man about whom the question of whether he was alive
or dead still hung in the air. Nor could they have guessed, that on

that very night, she would be granted the answer to that question.

At the end of the performance, Alexandra returned backstage, showered quickly, drank a glass of warm, spiced wine which waited for her on her make-up table, dressed in a comfortable, elegant suit, and prepared for her second mission every night – to entice the clients of the cabaret to invite her to drink champagne with them. She could not be convinced to give up this part of her work. It afforded an immediate assessment of how good her performance had been each night and flattered her femininity. Two members of the Gestapo sat in the club to make sure no rude, drunken officers harassed her.

"Table number four asked you to visit them…" said Michael, the club manager after the decorated SS officer who sat at the head of the table pressed a bill into his pocket.

Alexandra, more beautiful and radiant than ever, chatted with the guests in the club dense with the smell of sweat, alcohol, cigarette smoke, and perfume. She turned to the table to which she had been invited, where five officers of varying degrees of drunkenness sat. She approached them with a light step and a beaming smile, and suddenly stopped. Wearing an SS officer's uniform sat none other than the loathsome actor, Kurt Decker.

Kurt stood, clicked his heels, and with an exaggerated gesture, waved her over to sit with them. The other officers also stood, their looks of admiration and lust unmitigated. Alexandra wanted to run away, fast and far, but she summoned her strength and her acting skills, smiled broadly, and opened her arms. "Kurt Decker, Kurt Decker, my dear friend and colleague, it's been so long since I've seen you!"

Kurt, who had been afraid of how she would react to him, held her close and said, "Alexandra my dear, what a surprise to meet you here."

To those watching, they did in fact look like close friends who had been separated by the war; but looks can deceive. Kurt, from the first moment he saw the woman who had rejected him for a Jew, until she approached his table, had been busy plotting his ultimate revenge. He, who watched her on stage at the height of her skills, was not really impressed by how she fell into his arms like a lost brother.

After she chatted a little with the officers, Alexandra stood up to go to the next table. That was the moment that Kurt had been waiting for. He bent over her and whispered in her ear, "Do you remember Max Fischer?"

Alexandra could no longer hide the storm in her heart. "Why? Do you know how he is?" she asked in alarm.

"Yes, I can even arrange for you to meet him, if you're interested, of course."

Alexandra's heart skipped a beat. "I would be happy to meet him." With all the calm she could muster, she added, "I very much admired his talents as an actor."

"A clown, you mean as a clown," said Kurt. "Be ready to leave the day after tomorrow, in the afternoon. And bring a change of clothes in case you decide to stay with us overnight at the camp."

Alexandra parted from those seated, and quickly found herself whispering before the mirror backstage, "He's alive, my love is alive." For a moment, she was the happiest of people.

But sometimes, joy is paid for with great sorrow.

At table four, Kurt Decker got drunk off the admiration of his new friends and went back to exaggerating about how close he and Alexandra had been at the Berlin theater. The more wine was poured, the greater the heights to which his imagination soared. "I was the star, and she was my co-star," he said, "And there was also a Jewish actor named Max Fischer..."

"The one who makes the who's who of Munich laugh?" asked one of his cohorts.

"Yes, that's the one. In two days' time, I'm hosting a show at the camp. The baroness will also be there, you're all invited!"

"The son of your Jew, David Fischer, is at my camp," said one of the officers.

"Excellent, bring him with you," said Kurt.

# 4

From the first moment she heard about Max's imprisonment, Alexandra felt like a ray of sunshine was warming her face. While she waited for Iron, her thoughts danced in her head. She often wanted to ask Franz to find out if Max was alive, to calm herself, or at least to verify her worst fears, but she didn't dare so as not to hurt him or his dignity. And here, the good news had reached her from the last person she would have imagined could bring her good news. Not only did he know that Max was alive, he also employed him as a performer. Could it be that authority had in fact turned Kurt Decker into a better person, moderating his evil? Or was she endangering her life by accepting his invitation?

Iron stopped the car and hurried to open the door for her. He knew that something had her all worked up, but he avoided her eyes. Silence filled the car until they reached home.

"How was your evening, my dove?" asked Franz who was always awake when she arrived.

"A successful night," answered Alexandra. "I met an old friend, Kurt Decker, and he invited me to come to the camp which he commands."

"Yes, I know, talk to me tomorrow morning when you wake up," he answered.

Alexandra had stopped being surprised a long time ago by how he knew everything. She kissed his cheek, looked at him, and then put on her nightgown and lay down next to him. They had been sleeping side by side for many months now. In some sense, she loved him, loved to hug him, to absorb his warmth. He was strong, intelligent, and still gentle and considerate. If he would only ask, she would have been intimate with him - happily even. She fell into a deep sleep.

At six in the morning, Thomas woke her jumping on the bed. Franz had gotten up long ago to start his day. Alexandra quickly got herself organized and picked up the telephone receiver that was a direct connection to the Gestapo secretary. She asked for Franz. The secretary, who recognized her voice, transferred the conversation to his office, and from there to the commander.

"Yes, my beautiful," the soft voice of the most frightening man in Bavaria was heard. "Did you miss me?"

"Of course," answered Alexandra. On some level, it was true, and Franz knew it.

"Do you remember we spoke last night about the trip?" she asked.

"I remember every word you say, and every move you make," he said and added, "It's all arranged. Iron will take you there and bring you back. Now that the little bastard Kurt Decker knows who your man is, he won't dare to hurt a single hair on your head..."

# 5

When Franz returned from his workday, Alexandra sensed how overwrought he was. He poured them both a cognac and sat down across from her. Alexandra tensed.

"I was not straightforward with you," he said. "I know who Kurt Decker is, I know Max Fischer is imprisoned in the camp that he commands. It is also clear to me who Max is to you – the love of your life and Thomas' father…"

"You knew that Thomas was…" Alexandra had trouble finishing the sentence.

"Yes, of course, I knew. Immediately after my first visit to the Red Lantern, I had to investigate. And when I understood that he was the father, the secret you were hiding, and why you left the Berlin stage, I relaxed. With time, we have become closer to one another, and I have grown to love Thomas like my own son."

Alexandra sipped at her cognac in silence. "And I quickly realized who you are. I'm glad I chose you." Franz smiled. "Would it be too much to ask if you might be able to help him, maybe to free him?"

"You are so naïve, my Alexandra. Hitler and his men are systematically murdering every Jew in Europe. I have no power or ability to do anything against that…" Alexandra looked at him in silence. "But the end is close… very close. I'm happy to say, I believe Max will survive. Kurt makes money off his talent, enough money to make it worth keeping him alive." Franz gathered her up in his arms, and she held on to him tightly. Her lips found his.

"My love, I, I… I'm not very good at this…" he said trying to gently push her away, but she led him to bed, took off her clothes and his clothes and began to stroke him.

"I need you, I need your strength, now. Give it to me." His body responded in ways that it had failed him in the past, and when he penetrated her, and moved within her, nothing darkened his joy, not even the cry she made when she thrust her hips towards him, and her body trembled. "Max!" she cried, "Max!"

Franz studied her as she slept quietly, a smile sometimes rising to her lips. His heart beat as if it would burst from his chest. He was afraid of how she would react upon waking and seeing he was not her heart's love. After a long hour, she opened her blue eyes, and said, "Are you still awake, Franzie? Why did you wait so long?"

Franz lay next to her, stroked her face and neck with the back of his hand. "I am the happiest of men," he whispered. "I don't know why I am so lucky to have you, why you chose me. I don't deserve it. Not you and not any other prize... if you knew what I have done, what I do..."

She interrupted him, "Come here," she whispered, and he came.

## 6

Alexandra woke up late. Franz had already left for work and Thomas for school. She made herself a mug of coffee. On the table, a note was waiting for her. "We must speak, I'll come at lunchtime. Love, F."

Franz indeed came home at noon, his emotional turmoil evident in his expression. "I didn't tell you the whole truth, yesterday," he began without any introduction or preamble. "I am the investigating officer who caught Max Fischer. I never dreamt I would ever meet you, and I don't want this secret between us."

Alexandra took a deep breath and answered in a soft voice, "If it hadn't been you, another officer would have caught him. You are not the only detective in the Gestapo. You did your job. You did not mean to hurt me." She rested her head on his chest, quietly.

Franz felt a heavy weight lift from his shoulders, but he still hadn't said what was most important. "I want you to know that I have done horrible things in my position. I, whose mother is happily married to a Jew who raised me as the only father I have ever known, became part of a machine that, to this day, with the enemy at the gate, is busy trying to destroy the entire Jewish population. Just a minute, please, Alexandra, let me continue, I have to confess to someone, and there is no one else I can say this to. The Americans are within spitting distance from here. In another week or two they will conquer the whole area, and the nightmares that took place here and in Eastern Europe will be visible to the world. I cannot be caught and tried for my part in them. That mustn't happen, I will not let my mother and Avram know what I have done. The good Avram, my mother called him. And I cannot continue to live with the nightmares." He stopped his stream of speech for a moment. "Mother and Avram live in New York. When everything is over, please find them. I would prefer they don't know about my part in these horrific deeds – but that is your decision." Franz took a deep breath, and continued, "If it had not been for my love for you and for Thomas, I would not have made it until today. Iron will take you to the camp tomorrow. And immediately after leaving there, he will take you to Switzerland. Make sure to arrange a Nanny for Thomas. You don't have to worry, Iron has all the necessary travel passes.

"Switzerland?"

"Yes, it has to be tomorrow. There is a secret compartment in the car. After you cross the border, ask Iron to open it for you. There are two notebooks inside. In one are the details of my bank accounts and their secret numbers. You have power of attorney to do as you wish with the accounts. I added my mother and Avram's address. They don't need anything, except perhaps a picture of you and Thomas and me, our little family. There is also a list of all the properties, apartments, shops, the Lantern where we met – they are all already registered in your name. The deeds are in a safe in my home office. Alexandra, you are my sun and moon, the light of my eyes and the sound in my ears. I won't be able to take a thing with me where I am going." Alexandra fell into his arms with bitter tears. They held each other that way for a long time.

"The second notebook," he said, "please give to the Americans at the end of the war. The material recorded there will detail all of the horrors so that they can evaluate them and bring those responsible to justice. Keep Iron close to you, always. He will help you; he would sacrifice his life for you, if there's a need, and will tell you who is lying to you and who is speaking the truth, who is good and who is bad."

Franz went into his office and returned with a small package wrapped in a handkerchief. "Another thing. I want this bible that Avram gave me to guide you on your path. Who knows, maybe one day it will be helpful to you."

"I love you, Franz," Alexandra whispered and took the package from him. "Despite everything you have told me, I know you are a good person."

"Kiss Thomas for me, if I see him, I won't be able to leave him."

It would take Alexandra some time to digest all that Franz had told her and, until her dying day, she would not be able to understand how a man like him had been part of the most horrific killing machine in human history.

Franz left their house without looking back, and Alexandra knew she would never see him again.

"You won't leave me like he did, Uncle Iron, right?" was the only reference Thomas made to the man who had disappeared from his life. For over a year, he avoided mentioning his name, and stuck close to Iron.

# 7

When Franz finished instructing Iron, he asked to add a few personal words.

"I want you to know that in the long journey I have traversed in my life, you were the best choice I ever made. I am happy we walked this path together. You were an advisor to me, a confidant and, most significantly, a true friend. The only friend I ever had. And because of you, I got to be with Alexandra and Thomas."

Iron hugged him firmly, looked straight into his eyes and said, "I saw a look like the one in your eyes now, with my first dog. That night the old dog left and never returned."

"Iron, you good man, they..." Franz pointed around him, "bad mans. Very bad mans. You very strong; please protect our small family."

"Iron to protect Alexandra and Thomas with Iron's life," Iron also imitated the halting language he spoke at their first meeting, and his eyes grew moist.

# 1950, Munich, Circus Dantes

"I want us to take the circus to South America," said Max.

Alexandra, Iron, and Carlo all opened their mouths in harmony.

"Not an easy mission, boss," said Carlo. "You've got to sign contracts with local agents, get all the wagons and all the animals aboard a ship. The voyage itself will last weeks. And none of our performers will be able to practice and won't be in any shape to perform when we get there. They'll need at least a week of rehearsals and training…"

"Are you crazy?" said Alexandra, "We've performed in Germany, France, England. We have contracts to perform all over Europe. Why suddenly South America?"

"You are right, forgive me. I promise it's my last request to travel."

"And what about the existing contracts? It will cost us a ton to cancel them," added Carlo.

"We'll go after we've fulfilled them," answered Max.

Iron didn't say a word. He looked into Max's eyes and signaled Alexandra that he'd like to have a word with her.

"I don't know why… but it's something that comes from deep within him. It's a decision of his most primitive animal, or as the doctors say, his subconscious."

Alexandra sighed and asked Max to come with her to their wagon.

"I've received an offer to perform Shakespeare in London and for a role in an exciting musical on Broadway," she said and took a deep breath. "Come with me, we'll return to the stage. We'll leave the circus in Carlo's hands, and we'll start over. There's a lot more to our son than being an animal trainer..."

"Alex, this is my last insanity. Maybe, if I leave this dammed continent, I'll be rid of Kurt's crazy laugh that's chasing me day and night. I love you, and I am grateful for what you have done for me, but I will go with you or without you, with the circus or without it. Please come with me... You want a normal life? So do I. I can't explain it, but I have a strong feeling that my only chance for that kind of life, is hidden in South America."

Alexandra looked in his eyes for a long time. She didn't need Iron to see the plea within them. From that day, nearly four years passed before the circus had completed its commitments in Europe and boarded a ship to sail for Argentina.

# 1953, Buenos Aires, Circus Dantes

## 1

Many changes took place in the circus with its arrival in Buenos Aires. Some of the animals had been lent to another circus in Germany. Some of the artists decided not to take part in the journey, and Carlo auditioned local replacements. One of the first among them was Camilla, a woman of about forty years old, dark skinned and short, with facial features typical of the indigenous people of the Pampas. She was accompanied by her daughter of about sixteen, named Melina. Melina's skin was the color of honey, her body long and flexible, her eyes grey green, and her smile broke hearts.

Camilla impressed Carlo with her horsemanship, and he agreed to take her on.

"My daughter is better than I am," she said.

"She is only a girl," answered Carlo with a smile. But the mother would not give up and Carlo's curiosity was piqued. To his surprise, the girl chose the most powerful and energetic horse of them all, rubbed her nose against his, swung swiftly onto his back, and urged him into a gallop around the ring.

The horse leapt forward like a storm. The girl rested her head on his neck, stretched both her arms along his sides and raised her legs in the air. Thomas, who had by this time become a handsome young man, did not take his eyes off the wonder revealed before him. His heart raced. He was in love.

In the coming days, he would appear next to Milena when she stood next to her mother in line for food, smiled at her every moment he thought her eyes were turned to him, and tried to start a conversation with her. But Milena only politely smiled back at him. He was embarrassed to ask for advice on the matter from his mother or father, and Iron was busy up to his ears getting the circus in order in a new country. Aishé, who couldn't help but notice Thomas circling the Argentinian cowgirl, proposed that he come to her tent. He sat across from her, and she took his palm, stroked it, and looked at it with concentration.

"What about Milena?" he asked.

"What about her?" Aishé asked innocently and then smiled with understanding. "Oh, my sweet boy, I don't need to look at your palm to see you're in love with her. Patience, your feelings are strong. Right now, to Milena, everything is foreign, the place, the people, your language… Show her the animals you take care of. Ask her to teach you to ride like her. Love will come in its own time, don't pressure her."

"But how will I speak to her? I don't understand a word of Spanish."

"Love doesn't need words, Tommy, you'll understand each other. The problems will start when the talking starts."

They laughed. Aishé steeped a fragrant tea, and they drank it leisurely.

Thomas used his talents at pantomime to smooth a path to Milena's heart. They spent long hours side by side, demonstrating their abilities - she, riding horses, and he, communicating with animals. Before long, Thomas was happy to see the spark of love in her eyes.

## 2

"Straight from the plains of the Pampas, please welcome, Milena!" cried Carlo. The audience, discovering that the young rider was a fellow Argentinian, went wild.

In the evenings, Milena and Thomas were busy planning a joint performance. They used gestures to communicate what they wanted to express. "What are you thinking?" asked Thomas.

Milena brought her lips close to his and whispered, "Bésame, Thomas." Thomas kissed her. "Bésame," he whispered.

## 3

Circus Dantes became the hottest ticket in town throughout South America. Iron and Aishé were expecting a child, and Thomas – who was already taller than his father by half a head – blossomed. And Max developed a habit that worried Alexandra.

Two or three times a week, he would get out of bed in the middle of the night, put on make-up and leave the circus camp. Most of the time, he would return in the wee hours of the night, exhausted, and fall asleep the moment his head met the pillow.

Alexandra raised the issue with him. "I need a breath of air," he said, "And anyway, the laugh in my ears keeps me from sleeping…" She knew that wasn't the whole truth. Why did he get into costume? she asked herself.

It was a night like all the others. They had passionate sex, and when the sensual storm quieted, Max showered, made himself up, got dressed and went out, as was his habit. When she heard him return, she waited for him to get undressed and fall into bed, but this time, there was the sound of drawers opening, and running water in the bathroom. She opened the door and found him cleaning dried blood from his face.

"What happened?" she asked in fright.

"Nothing. I said to a handful of thugs that God is dead, and that got them mad. You know how they act after they've been drinking."

"Please stop, I'm not a child. Tell me what you're seeking at night, tell me why they attacked you. Is this what I need? To be afraid for your life?"

"I told you, drunken gentiles, that's all it was. They're not gonna kill me so easily." He presented his wounded fists proudly. "There were three of them, and one of me."

The next day, Alexandra gathered Iron and Thomas in her wagon and told them about the previous nights' events. "Iron, can you find out where he's going and what he's looking for there?"

"Of course, I'll go out after him and protect him."

"No, he can't know you're following him. He gets into costume, he doesn't want anyone to recognize him. And you, you're a little hard to hide. And you're identified with this circus…"

"Then I'll go."

The two adults looked at Thomas with surprise. They both reacted in more or less the same way, "You're too young for this kind of job."

"I'm sixteen. I beat almost all the adults here at wrestling…" Iron tried to interrupt, but Thomas raised his hand and said, "Let me finish, please. Like I said, I'm not a child, and I have Cheetah who is as good as three soldiers."

"Cheetah is not an attack dog. You think he could really protect you?" asked his mother.

"Cheetah would protect me even against you!"

The yellow dog, who was a wonder at entertaining children in the circus tent, pricked up his ears at the sound of his name. Suddenly, with no advanced warning, Alexandra erupted, screaming at Thomas and fell on him wildly. Before Thomas could even raise his hands to protect his face, the big dog stood over him and growled threateningly at Alexandra, who retreated.

"Cheetah, down! Mother, have you gone nuts?" Thomas cried.

Alexandra smiled. "I wanted to make sure he would indeed protect you, and I've been convinced that he will." She reached out to the dog who licked her happily.

The next night, Max went out on his walkabout again. Alexandra pressed on the electric switch that had been installed under her bed, ringing a bell in Thomas' room. Cheetah easily located Max's trail, and the two followed him at a safe distance.

"He hangs out at cheap, dark bars full of cigarette smoke," Thomas related the information when they returned. "He talks to people, invites them to drink..."

"And that's it? Are you sure?"

"It's hard for me to believe... but Papa is friends with neo-Nazis."

"You must mean the Hells Angels, that motorcycle gang."

"No Mama, Hells Angels don't have swastikas on their jackets."

# 1954, Santiago, Chile

## 1

After six months in Argentina, the circus traveled across the border to Chile, and pitched its tent in the capital city of Santiago. Praise for the circus had made its way from Argentina and the circus tent was already filled on opening night.

Alexandra finished her performance early and said she was tired and wanted to rest. Max went to their wagon and found her sleeping. He looked at her, his eyes traveling the length of her legs that were covered to her knee by a sheer, black nightgown. He gently touched her head and stroked her thick hair.

"You are so beautiful," he whispered almost to himself, "Like the first time I saw you. You have not changed at all."

Alexandra, who had learned to build an entire life on small moments of joy, arched her back. "Come to me, my man," she whispered, "Come to Alex."

Max kissed her toes and Alexandra twisted and moaned. He knew her body - where, when, and how much to press, to stroke, to pinch, to kiss, to bite. He flew to worlds where the laugh in his ears could not be heard, and when he climaxed, he felt as if his whole life force was gathered from the soles of his feet to the hair on his head. "I love you, Alex, I love you so much!" the cry emerged from his throat.

And then he waited quietly for her to fall asleep. He got up, carefully made himself up, put on Franz's wristwatch with the SS emblem engraved on its back, put on a white silk shirt, a grey suit, and a conservative tie.

"Heil Herr Gustav Mayer," he said to the character who was reflected back at him in the mirror and saluted him with a raised arm.

Alexandra reached for the electric switch and rang the bell in Thomas' wagon.

## 2

As quiet as a cat, Max left the circus camp. In his hand, he had a map of the city that had been marked with the addresses of bars where old Nazis gathered with local youngsters who had lost their way. A few minutes later, a tall youth emerged from his wagon, his yellow dog at his side.

As was customary in these kinds of bars, 'Vaterland' was dark and smoky. Young men with shaved heads visited the bar. More than one had a swastika tattooed on the top of his bald pate. Max smiled to himself bitterly. What do they have in common with Hitler's mad Reich? If only he could rest from the wild laugh in his ears. His eyes adjusted to the darkness and the thick smoke that burned them and scanned those present. All the cities he visited, all the libraries whose collections he looked through, all the cafes he sat in and the dark bars he drank in over the last few years, had led him to this particular bar in Chile. But he didn't really know if this place would take him even one step closer to his goal.

Max sat at an open table next to a loud group of young Nazis and signaled to the waiter. He ordered a bottle of schnapps, a shot glass, and a pint of Lowenbrau. The waiter realized his customer had money to spend and brought the drinks quickly. Max filled the shot glass with schnapps. He raised it in the air, smiled at whomever stood in front of him, and emptied its contents down his throat. Then, he lifted the heavy glass of beer, drank from it with pleasure, put it back down on the table with a bang and joined in humming with the march that played over the speakers.

After three rounds, the laugh in his ears had diminished. He grabbed the bottle and stood up heavily like a drunk. He approached the table next to him and asked in a hoarse voice, "Schnapps?" The young men responded happily and signaled the waiter to bring over another chair. Max poured a round, raised his glass, and cried, "Heil the Fatherland!" They emptied their glasses, roared, "Heil Hitler" in response, and Max poured another round. He never forgot the rules of the game. To an onlooker, he looked like a middle-aged German, drunk and enjoying the moment.

After about an hour, a conversation developed around the table, in Spanish. Max added a heavy German accent to his speech.

"Where are you from?" he was asked.

"From the Fatherland."

"And what did you do then, in the big days?"

"I served the Führer in the service of the SS," he said. One of the youths, who looked like the leader of the group, casually shook Max's hand, and looked for the tattoo that SS officers emblazoned on themselves.

"I had to have it removed. Jews today are everywhere, you know how it is," he said and proudly displayed the SS symbol etched on his watch.

The neo-Nazi nodded and roared, "The day will come when we take the world back from the communists and Jews, and we'll wear the symbol of the unit with pride..."

Max nodded and raised his glass. He wanted to shake him and roar in his ear, "Have you heard of Kurt Decker? Tell me where he is!" But he could not blink first, he mustn't be seen as someone looking for something. He continued with the performance of his life which he had now enacted dozens, if not hundreds of times, in the lead role. But the sets, the dark bars, the costumes and the make-up, the audience, the language, the countries – it all changed. It was his job to continue the game and wait for an opportunity.

"And you?" asked a young man whose pristine mustache decorated his pock-marked face, "Did you see any action? Tell us…" Max looked at him, and for a naïve moment again wondered why a young man his age, would connect to the complete evil that ruled on another continent, in another age. Max quoted the name of the camp where he had been imprisoned. "And what's your name?" asked the young man.

Max signaled for his new friends to lean in closer and asked, "I'm among friends, I can talk here, right?" Once they had responded positively, he said, "My name is Gustav Mayer."

"And what did you do in the camp, Herr Mayer?" someone asked. Max looked around angrily. "Please call me Michael Hertz," he said. "Who knows who's listening…" And then added, "I was the deputy commander of the camp."

"While Kurt Decker was commander?" shot back the young man.

Max was not prepared for the question and blanched. "I see you are a well-connected and smart young man. Very good, we need men like you, but I won't give you names either."

Max put his head down on the table as if he were felled by the schnapps and beer. He needed time to organize his thoughts, but his brain was thinking of leaping from his skull. His heart pounded so fast and hard he was afraid his friends at the table could hear it. Max felt very close to his prey. He had to act quickly, to reach him, wrap his hands around his neck and strangle him to death. He would not be free of the laugh in his head as long as Kurt Decker was alive.

Kurt Decker had to die, so that Max could live.

## 3

Only a few minutes away, in one of the circus's sleeping wagons, Aishé woke up in a panic. She shook Iron who lay next to her and yelled, "Go help him, they're going to attack him. I see death, save him!"

Iron was startled awake. "Aishé, you're pregnant, you mustn't have these feelings, calm down, it's only a bad dream."

"Run, take the dog, and find them. They're there, both father and son, the others have weapons."

Aishé blessed the good luck that led her to adopt Laima, a stray dog who followed them some years before from the center of Berlin to the circus. A good-natured dog, loyal, and strong. Iron whistled to her and sent her after Cheetah.

## 4

With Max and Thomas' departure from the circus encampment, Alexandra sat on the steps of her wagon. She lit a cigarette, inhaled the smoke deeply, and stubbed the cigarette out in an ashtray. The door of the wagon next to hers opened. Iron ran out with his dog. She lit the cigarette again, saw Aishé leave the wagon and stand with eyes closed. A cry in an unintelligible language rose from her throat.

She approached the wailing Aishé. "What happened, Aishé, why did Iron go out?" she asked.

"Pray, my sister," answered Aishé, "Pray to whoever you believe in. Pray to him to protect our loved ones."

## 5

The young man who sat across from Max went to the telephone next to the bar, exchanged a few words with someone on the other end of the line, and returned to the table. He whispered something into the ears of his friends. Max witnessed the exchange of words but did not know what was said. He also did not notice as they each left one after the other, and returned to the table a short time later. If he had been focused, maybe he would have been more careful and not followed happily after them. But he felt so close to his target, and had drunk quite a bit, his senses were blunted. "Come see your surprise," said the leader of the group, and they advanced together towards the door of the bar.

Only once he stood in the entranceway, two thugs behind him and three in front, did Max realize he had been led like a lamb to the slaughter.

"Who do you work for? Are you Israeli? From the Mossad?" cried the leader.

"No, no, I'm running from them, just like all the rest of us…" answered Max. His well-trained body tensed when he saw the drawn knives, the clubs, and the bicycle chain that flashed in the hands of one of them.

"Gustav Mayer died two years ago. And don't you worry, by the time we're done with you, you'll tell us who you really are, who you work for, who your partners are, and what shoe-size your father wears."

Max leaped forward and punched the speaker hard in the face, and then he turned around and tried to escape between the two who were standing behind him. The blow that landed on the back of his neck knocked him to the ground. He felt boots kicking him.

Twenty meters away, in a dark alley, stood a young man watching the entrance of the bar. The door opened and closed, human filth entered upright and exited swaying, throwing their guts up and loudly singing songs from an era he didn't know. Sometimes, like the group that exited the bar at that particular moment, they fought amongst themselves wildly.

Thomas was daydreaming about the girl waiting for him in his bed and had lost his focus, but the threatening sound that escaped Cheetah's throat made it clear it was his father who was knocked to the ground. Thomas shot forward, and Cheetah attacked the first attacker in front of him. The man fell forward, and Cheetah went after the one behind him. He caught him by the genitals and pulled him out of the way while he screamed. Thomas leapt on another skinhead and grabbed his neck while Cheetah sunk his teeth into his thigh and pulled him back. The skinhead stabbed Cheetah in the back – Cheetah did not let go.

Thomas and his father were positioned against the last two attackers, who began to retreat. But the door of the bar flew open, and three more neo-Nazis burst out, ready and eager to fight.

While father and son stood ready to fight their losing battle, there was the sound of barking. Iron grabbed two of the attackers, slammed them against each. Laima caught the third. The two who were left ran for their lives.

"Papa, are you okay?" Thomas asked fearfully.

"Let's get out of here, there are at least two dead here, they mustn't recognize us," cried Iron. The three men and Laima moved quickly, with Iron carrying the bleeding Cheetah on his shoulders.

"How did you get here?" Max asked his son.

"Cheetah and I have been following you since the first time you were attacked. I'm so sorry I wasn't focused… I'm ashamed I reacted so slowly…"

"What are you ashamed of? Saving my life? Come here, my son," he put his hand on his shoulder, "Your nose is swollen and you have a black eye. Tomorrow, you can perform as a clown with no need for make-up." Max's joking broke the tension and they all laughed.

"What about Cheetah?" asked Thomas.

"A superficial wound," said Iron, and Cheetah responded with happy barks. They strode through the silence back to the circus grounds. When they arrived, Thomas and Iron sewed up Cheetah's wounds and took care of Thomas' face. Max continued toward his wagon with the hope that Alex would be fast asleep. She was wide awake.

# 6

Max found her sitting on the steps of the wagon, holding a picture of him and Thomas and praying quietly.

"Where is Thomas?" she asked immediately. "If he lost a single hair on his head, you've taken your life in your own hands!"

"He's okay," said Max. "And he didn't save my life so that you could take it." They entered the wagon, and she took care of his bruised face. "I don't know who you fought, and I don't want to know," she said. "I'm leaving. Tomorrow I'm buying a plane ticket. I'm taking Thomas with me."

"Alex, please, I promised you this was the last city, stay."

"No. Tomorrow I'm buying tickets to New York for Thomas and me. I'm sorry, I can't take this tension anymore."

"Alex, my love, I am so sorry that I am not the man you waited for. You took me into your home, you took care of me like a friend, a mother, a lover, and a merciful nurse, all at once. You created this circus for me, and you sacrificed your career for it. And what have I given you in return?" Alexandra, stunned, hugged and kissed him. "I have not given you anything, Alex, except sorrow and grief. I will not try to force you to stay with me, but I feel so close to my target. Maybe I will finally understand the demons that are driving me, I need a little more time."

Alexandra finished treating his face and kissed him. "You gave me a lot, Max. You believed in me, you made room for me on the stage beside you, you allowed me to shine unlike any other actress, I knew it even then. And still, I cannot stay here. Finish what you need to do and come back to me. I will wait for you, my love." She got undressed and got into bed.

At dawn, she went to Thomas' wagon. She sat next to him and looked at his battered but peaceful face.

"What are you doing here?" he asked when he woke up and sensed her by his side.

"What mothers do, my child, worry about their babies. I could have lost you... Thomas, we are leaving the circus, I can't do this anymore, I almost lost you both. Today I am ordering us tickets to fly to New York. We'll take the first flight out of here."

"Mama, I understand why. But please, give me another month. I'll come with Papa," said Thomas. "One more month. I promise he won't leave the circus at night. Iron, Cheetah, and I will make sure of it."

## 7

The next afternoon, Alexandra had a ticket to New York in hand. She asked to gather the whole circus for a conversation in the big tent. Except for Thomas and Max, not one of them knew the purpose of the meeting.

"I want to thank all of you, each and every one individually," she said, "for your personal contribution to the tremendous success of this circus that has sprouted from your talents and from our connection to one another as a family. You are all my family, I love you." She lifted her hand to stop the rustling that rose from the circus people and added, "I'm leaving the circus, but not leaving you, you are in my heart forever. I am grateful to you, and I am instructing Carlo to give you each a bonus of a month's salary as a parting gift from me. Thank you, and I am sure we will meet again."

Later, in their wagon, she parted from Iron and Aishé. "There are no words to describe what I feel and think about you, Iron. I know that in all the years that we have known each other, you have avoided looking in my eyes and examining my 'animal.' I would appreciate if you would do that now."

Iron looked in her eyes and tears came to his own. "It's a shame you don't know how to read me," he said. "You would see in my eyes the love I see in yours." Alexandra wiped away her tears. And she said to Aishé, "maybe I won't be here with the birth of your baby, but our being apart is temporary. We will return and see one another. You are my dear family, and I will not give you up."

Aishé studied her palm closely. "Of course, Alexandra, I see we still have a future together. We'll meet again soon."

"May I make one final request?" Alexandra asked her.

"Of course," answered Aishé.

"I will miss your coffee so much," she said smiling.

Aishé smiled, went to the cabinet, and took out the small finjan and a large tin of coffee grounds with cardamom. "I don't need Iron's skills to understand what you want," she said.

The three burst into freeing laughter.

# 1945, Camp Kaufering, Bavaria

## 1

"I have sad news for you," Kurt said to Max. "As you know, the Reich is transferring Jews from its territory to Eastern Europe for resettlement. But your wife and parents didn't survive the journey and died on the way."

Max wanted to yell, to cry, to tear away the beard stuck to his face, to rend his clothes, but he gave nothing away.

"Maybe you know what happened to my son, David?" he asked.

"He is still alive," smiled Kurt.

"Then I have a good reason to make you laugh today," said the Jew decisively and rose from his chair. Kurt was disappointed. He hadn't expected such self-control, but he took comfort in knowing the whole evening was still before them and, at the end of that evening, Max Fischer's stone-faced mask would be removed.

"Tonight, I have special guests," said Kurt. "The show must be funnier than ever."

This pig wants a funny show. I'll give him a funny show. I will fuck him and everything he symbolizes on stage, and they will laugh. This idiot will laugh, too, without realizing that he himself is the pig on stage. That's what the pig asked for, that's what the pig will get.

# 2

After a half hour drive, Alexandra reached the Kaufering camp. Kurt waited for her at the entrance, his face beaming. He invited her for a light meal and served her chilled white wine in a sweating glass. A door opened and Max entered, thin and bearded, in a clean prison uniform. Their eyes met, and they hugged. "You have a son from me, just as handsome as you," she whispered in his ear.

"We're here." Iron's voice interrupted her dream. The black Mercedes pulled quietly through the open gates of the camp. Alexandra quickly shook herself and fixed her make-up. As the guard at the gate directed Iron where to park, Max brought his choir of coughers on stage. A subordinate officer instructed Alexandra to follow him. Iron strode several yards behind them, not taking his eyes off her. The officer opened the door of the hall and signaled for Alexandra to enter and for Iron to stay outside. Alexandra entered the ballroom with confident steps but was not prepared for what lay before her eyes.

# 1954, Circus Dantes

Max sat looking in the mirror, just as he had thousands of times over the previous years, seeing-not-seeing the eyes that stared back at him. The cheers of the merry audience, the thunder of the drums, the blare of the trumpets, and the low oompah of the tubas - none of it penetrated the wall insulating his senses.

At that moment, his whole world was focused on the one repetitive action he executed once, sometimes twice a day, day after day, week after week, year after year.

In precise concert with the moment he finished applying his make-up, the excited call of the ring master could be heard in the background, "Please welcome the funniest clown in the world, the man who has made more children laugh than anyone else in history. No one knows from where he came or to where he is going... Here's - Anonymous!"

Max thrust his hand out at the silent toy clown and knocked him onto his face, covered his own nose with a red rubber ball, stood up, and strode towards the circus ring. The roar of the crowd, the cheers of the children, and the sounds of the noisy circus orchestra reached his ears. But through it all, in the background, from some undefined direction, he also heard the sound that accompanied him day and night, through wakefulness and dreams, the sound that never let up:

the pealing wails of the crazy laugh. Max tried not to listen to the laugh. He focused on the noise of the great drums, boom, boom, boom. His stride began to melt into their rhythm. With every step that brought him closer to the ring, Max grew lighter, more flexible. He was again transformed into a clown, into Anonymous.

From the moment Anonymous burst into the rollicking circus ring – nothing was left of Max or of anything else – even the crazy laugh was nearly silenced. Except for the dead eyes that ceaselessly scanned the crowd as if searching for something lost, there was barely anything that connected Max to Anonymous the Clown, who elicited howls of laughter and tears of joy with the skill of an artist. And this was exactly what he was about to do now. Make people laugh.

Cheetah chased him and he ran away, screaming "Help!" at the top of his lungs. Suddenly, like a nightmare taking hold in the dead of night, he heard the mad laugh thundering in his ears. His hand, about to throw the large bone to the dog, froze. He tried covering his ears to focus on the thing he was practiced at, to entertain, to elicit laughter. The noise of the circus dimmed, and with it, the laugh. He lowered his hands from his ears, and then covered them again, released and covered and released them again feverishly, to be sure that the laugh did not come from his damaged mind but from outside him, from the audience. And it was, in fact, the very laugh he had been waiting for since the circus was established.

All these years he knew that, even if Kurt dyed his hair or changed his face with some kind of device or surgery, he would not be able to change his laugh. A spark that had been lost years ago returned to his eyes, the same eyes that searched the audience at every circus performance, in every dark bar. But this time, he had a sound to focus on. His eyes sought the man who produced the harrowing laugh. Cheetah realized something had happened to his master. He tried to stop but slid in the dirt of the ring and slammed into the clown's knees, the clown who beat at his own ears. Anonymous stumbled, completed a perfect summersault and returned to his feet.

The mad laugh was clear and powerful. Max's eyes focused on the third row, to the right of the aisle. There, next to a young woman and a small child, sat Kurt Decker. His eyes darkened. Again, he fell backwards and again, jumped lightly to his feet.

Suddenly, there was an opening in the foggy curtain that whisked him back a full decade, and from within him emerged the figure of Kurt Decker in his pressed SS uniform, standing next to a Jewish boy in rags and pointing a pistol at him. Kurt laughs, and Alexandra, so beautiful, yells while her hand covers her open mouth.

Focus, he said to himself. You have planned for this moment, you have waited for it, you have rehearsed for it. An entire circus was established for this very purpose! You didn't miss a single performance in order not to miss this moment. And here he is, Kurt Decker, right in front of you. His face had aged, heavy glasses hid his eyes, but it is he, the murderer who ruined your life, and he is laughing his crazy laugh, the laugh that has finally trapped him in your hands! Max froze in place as if suddenly paralyzed - exactly as he had then, at that last performance when clarity struck and sliced through his mind.

# 1945, Camp Kaufering, Bavaria

Max was satisfied. The SS officers and their girlfriends and wives laughed loudly. This was the moment to bring out the new toy that Laizer the carpenter made for him. Here is the cart with the long handle that is tied to me with a belt, and on it stands a stuffed Nazi pig – made of pink rags with the rank of a major in the SS, it's very funny.... Oy Laizer, Laizer, what a pig you made for me, a pig more piggish than those created by He who created pigs... Let's go... Leaning forward, as if the wagon were heavy, Max strained. Pulled the wagon like peddlers pull a loaded cart... They're laughing. Here's the crazy laugh. They saw the cart, and they saw the pig... "*Alte zachen!*" Yes, this cry of the ragman is killing them... Get closer to them, close half an eye like in the caricatures of Jews and ask, "What's funny about a Jew with a cart full of rags?" He straightened his back and yelled, now... "*Vas machsta!*" Ha... they understand Yiddish and are rolling with laughter. Now peek over your shoulder. Not that way Max – in a big movement – this is not the theater, it's a circus. Exaggerate. Overdo it. Wonderful. They are beside themselves. It works. Now the pig runs away. Chase it, and now in a large voice, "*Gevalt, a pig, a hazer.*" Oh, how it makes them laugh. I wonder who the special guests are. Run, Max, run from the pig who wears Kurt's rank. He won't understand the symbolism, I could have left it out, but my friends in the barracks will laugh so hard... And it's time I laugh too... I stop... the pig stops... a finger to my lips. They are quiet. Excellent. Turn around carefully, let the handle slip off the belt. Here I look at the pig. Shhh... everyone is quiet, and I start to push the cart and run after the pig. "Stop, you little piggy! I want to tell you something." The pig runs away again and again it makes them laugh. "Stop already, I won't hurt you! On matters of principle and morality I don't eat your kind." I lower the handle and the pig stops. Now jump on him from behind and thrust forward and back like a village shepherd having intercourse with his sheep. Fuck the animal, Max, fuck this German pig! The commandant and his pig friends laugh like they've never laughed before. Turn the pig over on the ground and jump on it, Max. What ecstasy, what a wonderous life.

Alexandra hears the resounding laughter. She strides lightly into the ballroom, but the show revealed before her eyes is a blow to her heart. She looks reluctantly at the grotesque display. The caricature of the man on the stage looks at her, and she screams, "Max!" His eyes meet her frightened ones. His lips part but no sound comes out. Max freezes in place, his muscles do not answer him. Alexandra? My beautiful Alex? What is she doing here? She mustn't see me like this... She cannot recognize me... I cannot move, I cannot utter a word. Leave Alex! Go, please! You must not see me this way. Go! Alex! She doesn't hear me. Alexandra yells, "What are you trying to tell me, Max?"

Max continues to look at her and cannot get a sound out. Snap out of it, he thinks, you must! You know what will happen if you don't make them laugh. Wait, why is there a Jewish child here? Who is this child? Where did he come from? Wait, Kurt, I will be funny, don't kill the child, he is only a child, what has he done to you? Why a pistol? Why can't you hear me…? Why is everyone laughing, wait I will make you laugh, here I'm jumping on the pig, just leave him alone. Alexandra is here, this must truly be hell. Go! I can't move while you're looking at me like this, you don't understand what will happen if I'm not funny… Kurt, leave the boy alone, take me, shoot me! God, someone, help me, why doesn't anyone hear? And suddenly, clarity slices through his mind. "Bastard! Don't shoot my son!" he yells full-throated, attacking Kurt with his bare fists. A blow of the gun to the back of his neck stops him. He falters forward, one step, then another, and a shot pierces the air. Max falls on the bleeding body of his son.

"What did I do?!" "What did I do?!" yelled Alexandra and collapsed to the ground.

Iron, who all this time stood outside the ballroom, burst in with a kick of the door, pushed the guard aside and rushed to his mistress. Before anyone moved a finger, he lifted her on his shoulders and carried her to the back seat of the Mercedes. The car lurched forward, breaking the barrier at the gate.

"What did I do?" murmured, Alexandra. "I killed his son…"

"You are not guilty of anything," said Iron. "Decker never considered leaving his son alive." But Alexandra didn't listen. Iron drove quickly toward Switzerland to fulfill Franz's last request.

# 1954, Chile, Circus Dantes

Again, Max stood like a statue, paralyzed, just as he had been then, in front of the man who had aimed a pistol at his son's head. Suddenly, it was as if something exploded inside him. He lifted his head to the sky and shouted his grief and pain, wailed the cursed guilt that had been eating at his heart and soul these last ten years, and had stolen his memory. Why did I freeze then? Why didn't I make them laugh? I killed my son! Max screamed in his heart. The audience started to laugh hesitantly. Cheetah, who for the second time in two days, raced to save his master, sat on his hind legs, looked at the sky and let out a cry that was louder than Max's. The hesitant laughter of the audience, turned into cheers.

But although the audience returned to the clown, Max did not return to the audience. Nor did Anonymous, whose existence ended the moment Max heard the laugh in his ears and not in his imagination. Cheetah, who smelled the fear that mingled with his sweat, jumped on him, knocking him to a seated position and began to lick his face, smearing his make-up. Max, pulled himself together, stood up and pulled the large bone out of his huge pants and threw it across the ring. Cheetah raced after it, and Max called to the audience, "I'm not afraid of him…" But Max was not Anonymous whose whole heart was attuned to the audience. He was a theater actor who finally got to fulfill the role of his life, the role which he had practiced and executed in his head over and over thousands of times. He would come to Kurt, grab him by the throat and squeeze. And before Kurt took his last cursed breath, he would command him, "Laugh, Commandant, laugh! I will make you laugh for the last time in your life!"

He approached his enemy slowly. The audience continued to laugh. Max, confused and excited, was funnier than Anonymous, and what he left out – the dog filled in. From the moment his master did not interfere and did not give him any commands, Cheetah fell over whining, he barked and ran away, jumped and failed, fell and bit his own tail wildly. And while Max and Cheetah, or more precisely Cheetah and Max, each gave the performance of their lives, each in his own way, a young man stood in his usual place next to the ring, terrified. He loved Max. He knew his father as a clown, and also as a cynical man, disconnected from his surroundings, but his senses screamed that something strange was taking place before his eyes. When his father looked up and screamed heavenward, Thomas felt for the first time in his life, true horror. Cheetah, who also took part in the wailing, did not fool him. I hope mother hasn't left yet, he thought and raced out of the tent.

Alexandra was already sitting in a taxi, while Iron loaded her suitcase into the trunk.

"Mama, come fast, Papa has gone crazy..." he cried.

"Thomas, I have a flight in three hours, we talked about everything. Everything is agreed upon...."

"Mama, I tell you something is happening, and I don't know what. His eyes... he changed the whole show... something took control of him. Mama, I'm scared, please come!"

Alexandra got out of the car, held onto her son's shoulders and shook them firmly. "What else did you see? Tell me."

"There's... there's someone there with a crazy laugh," answered Thomas.

Alexandra ran toward the tent and Iron ran after her. So that was what he was searching for all those years, thought Alexandra. He finally found Kurt Decker. May God help us.

The mayhem in the circus tent had reached its peak. Max rode on a unicycle through the audience, while Cheetah distributed surprises to the children. They both stopped in front of a man, a woman, and child.

A son. He has a son. An eye for an eye. A son for a son. The clown with the wide smile and shining eyes leaped forward and pushed his painted face inches away from Kurt's face. "*Hijo?*" asked the voice that was heard through the entire tent. The father smiled proudly and answered, "*Mi hijo,*" without knowing that with those two innocent words – "my son" – he determined his fate. Max reached out to the boy, and they walked leisurely to the center of the ring. "An eye for an eye, a son for a son." Max murmured. "There is nothing more just in the world than that."

Walking nonchalantly in his Charlie Chaplin gate, Max released the cables of the safety net, and again held his hand out to the boy. Together they climbed the steps of the ladder jauntily.

"No! Leave the boy!" yelled Alexandra when she entered the ring, but the clown and the boy were already swinging on the high trapeze. Alexandra's panicked cry distracted the cheering crowd. Kurt immediately realized who she was and then, who the clown was. He stood up in dread.

Alexandra held onto Thomas' hand. They approached the ladder and tried to talk to Max, but he only stared at Kurt, and called in a voice heard from one side of the circus to the other, "Laugh, Commandant Decker, laugh! Why aren't you laughing?! I haven't forgotten how to make Nazi officers laugh! Laugh! It would be a shame for your son to die!"

Loud cries rose from the audience. Some of the circus people climbed the ladder, others began to stretch the safety net under the trapeze, but Max called in a threatening voice, "Silence!"

He held the boy's hand with one hand, and when the boy hung between heaven and earth, he said, "If you get closer to me or touch the net, we both will fall." All the circus people moved aside except Iron who stood under the trapeze. Max turned to the audience, pointed at Kurt, and in a monotone, in Spanish, as if he were reading a sentence in a court of law, Max told about the camp, about the people who were murdered under the command of Kurt Decker, about Herschel who was shot because he, the clown, wasn't funny enough, about Motl the Pole who died of exhaustion and hunger, about the abuse, and about himself, about the role Kurt imposed on him. His face dripped with sweat. His strength failed. "And one time, I failed, I froze, I was not funny." His voice broke. "I'm sorry, David. Forgive me, my little one, I tried, I truly tried, I couldn't make him laugh... and he..." Max fought his voice. "He shot my son, before my eyes, he shot him and laughed. Yes. He laughed!"

Max looked at the boy in his grasp who was crying bitterly. "And since then, I am funny, I make everyone laugh, I have to... so no more children die. Not even his son... Laugh, Commandant Decker, Laugh!"

And Kurt began to laugh.

"No!" raged Max, "Not a laugh like that! Laugh the laugh I hear in my ears at every moment, every hour, when I sleep, when I am awake, when I eat. Laugh your evil laugh, so I know I am not just imagining it all these years! Laugh, Kurt, laugh so your son won't..."

And Kurt laughed, and his laugh tore through the silent tent. He laughed like he had never laughed in his life, a crazy laugh that burst from his heart and passed through his throat. That terrible laugh returned Max to a different moment, in a different world when he stood shocked and silent in front of his abuser, in front the woman he loved, and in front of David, his son. To the moment in which he knew that the life of his son was dependent on the laugh that was produced in the throat of this man - and failed. And here was this man in front of him again, and his beloved woman, and the boy in his hands.

"David, do you hear?" Max looked at the whimpering child. "David, he's laughing, I didn't freeze, I succeeded in making him laugh, you've been saved, David. Why are you crying my son? Listen, it's all okay, I did it...." Max pulled the strange child to him, wrapped him in his arms and whispered in his ear, " Sshhh, David, Shhhh, don't cry, clowns don't hurt children, clowns are funny... don't cry, my son."

While Max hugged the boy, and murmured calming words in his ear, Thomas hurried to climb the rungs of the ladder, and took the boy in his arms. The three climbed down the ladder together.

Thomas turned the boy over to his mother, and Max – in whose ears Kurt's crazy laugh no longer echoed – fell into Alexandra's arms. "Let's go home," he whispered to her. "It's time."

They paid no attention to the two policemen who arrested Kurt Decker and led him to the nearest police station. And no one noticed the young man who walked silently after them with his dog.

"Maybe Papa forgave you," Thomas whispered to himself, "but I will not let you laugh ever again."

And Thomas released his dog.